PRINT'S BEST LOGOS & SYMBOLS

Published by RC Publications, Inc.
104 Fifth Ave.,
New York, NY 10011

Manufactured in Hong Kong

PRINT'S BEST LOGOS & SYMBOLS

Library of Congress Catalog Card
Number 89-091068
ISBN 0-915734-65-6

RC PUBLICATIONS

President and Publisher: Howard Cadel
Vice President and Editor: Martin Fox
Creative Director: Andrew Kner
Managing Editor: Tom Goss
Associate Art Director: Thomas Guarnieri

Second Printing

Print's Best
LOGOS & SYMBOLS
WINNING DESIGNS FROM PRINT MAGAZINE'S NATIONAL COMPETITION

Edited by
TOM GOSS

Art Directed by
ANDREW KNER

Designed by
THOMAS GUARNIERI

Published by
RC PUBLICATIONS, INC.
NEW YORK, NY

INTRODUCTION

The origins of what are now called logos and symbols have been traced to a medieval law requiring bakers to mark their wares so that those selling underweight loaves could be identified and prosecuted. Similar laws applied to other craftsmen, particularly gold- and silversmiths, and the penalties for selling falsely marked wares were quite severe. Later, as manufacturing became more of a collective endeavor in the industrialized age, these personal marks evolved into trademarks which were also registered and protected by law.

Little is known about the marks originally placed on loaves of bread, as the loaves were no doubt eaten, but the marks of craftsmen and their industrialized descendants were chiefly characterized by their pictorial quality. The products these trademarks stood for were readily identifiable, since they depicted the products themselves or other objects associated with those products. As the business of manufacturing—and business in general—became more complex, however, companies needed symbols that not only identified their products (which in a modern corporation could be as diverse as electronics and party snacks), but also the corporation as an entity unto itself. It was out of this need that the modern logo, or as the dictionary would have it, "logotype," was born. (Indeed, the definitions of "trademark" and "logotype" reflect this evolution: *The American Heritage Dictionary* defines trademark as a symbol or name used to identify a company's product, while a logotype is defined as a symbol or name that identifies a particular company *or* its product.) Logos in recent times became more symbolic and abstract than their trademark ancestors, as graphic designers, who were now responsible for creating them, were instructed to design the marks to communicate the corporations' philosophies and goals, rather than simply

CONTENTS

what products they made or what services they provided.

As the logos and symbols collected in this volume indicate, however, this trend toward abstraction doesn't apply to the overall field of logo design. The vast majority of the marks presented here were designed for individual professionals, craftspersons and small, service-oriented businesses that make up a growing portion of the American economy. These businesses and professionals, like the craftsmen of old, not only want to project a distinct identity for themselves and their enterprises, but also a human, friendly personality. For that reason, many of the logos and symbols in this book are more pictorial than abstract, and many even resemble 19th-century trademarks.

Most of the 224 logos and symbols reproduced on these pages were designed for clients who run the gamut from large corporations to individuals. There are also marks designed for one-time-only special events. All of the marks shown here were previously published in past editions of PRINT's Regional Design Annual, which is itself the result of a national design competition judged by the editors and art director of PRINT magazine. The logos and symbols are reproduced larger than they appeared in the Annual (indeed, larger than they appear in actual use in many cases), and where such material was available, they are presented with some of their applications. The logos, symbols and their applications are not organized into arbitrary thematic groupings, but rather are presented in a sequence designed to entertain and to provide some creative insight. We believe that this approach makes the book visually stimulating as well as a useful reference tool for the designer. —*Tom Goss*

Bruce Hands, Photographer

DESIGN FIRM: Hornall Anderson Design Works, Seattle, Washington

ART DIRECTOR: Jack Anderson

DESIGNERS: Jack Anderson, Cliff Chung, Rey Sabado

ILLUSTRATOR: Cliff Chung

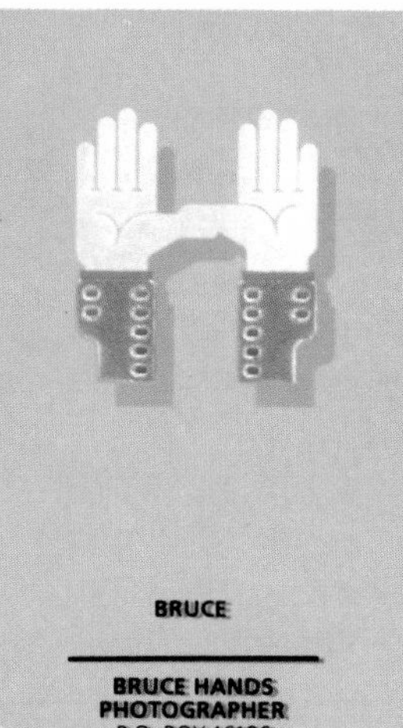

DELIVERY AGREEMENT

BRUCE HANDS
PHOTOGRAPHER
P.O. BOX 16186
SEATTLE, WA 98116-0186
(206) 938-8620

To:

Quantity	Format	Subject

Terms & Conditions reverse side.

Please check count and acknowledge by signing and returning one copy. Count will be considered accurate and quality deemed satisfactory if copy is not immediately received with exceptions noted.

Acknowledged and accepted subject to terms and conditions.

Signed Date

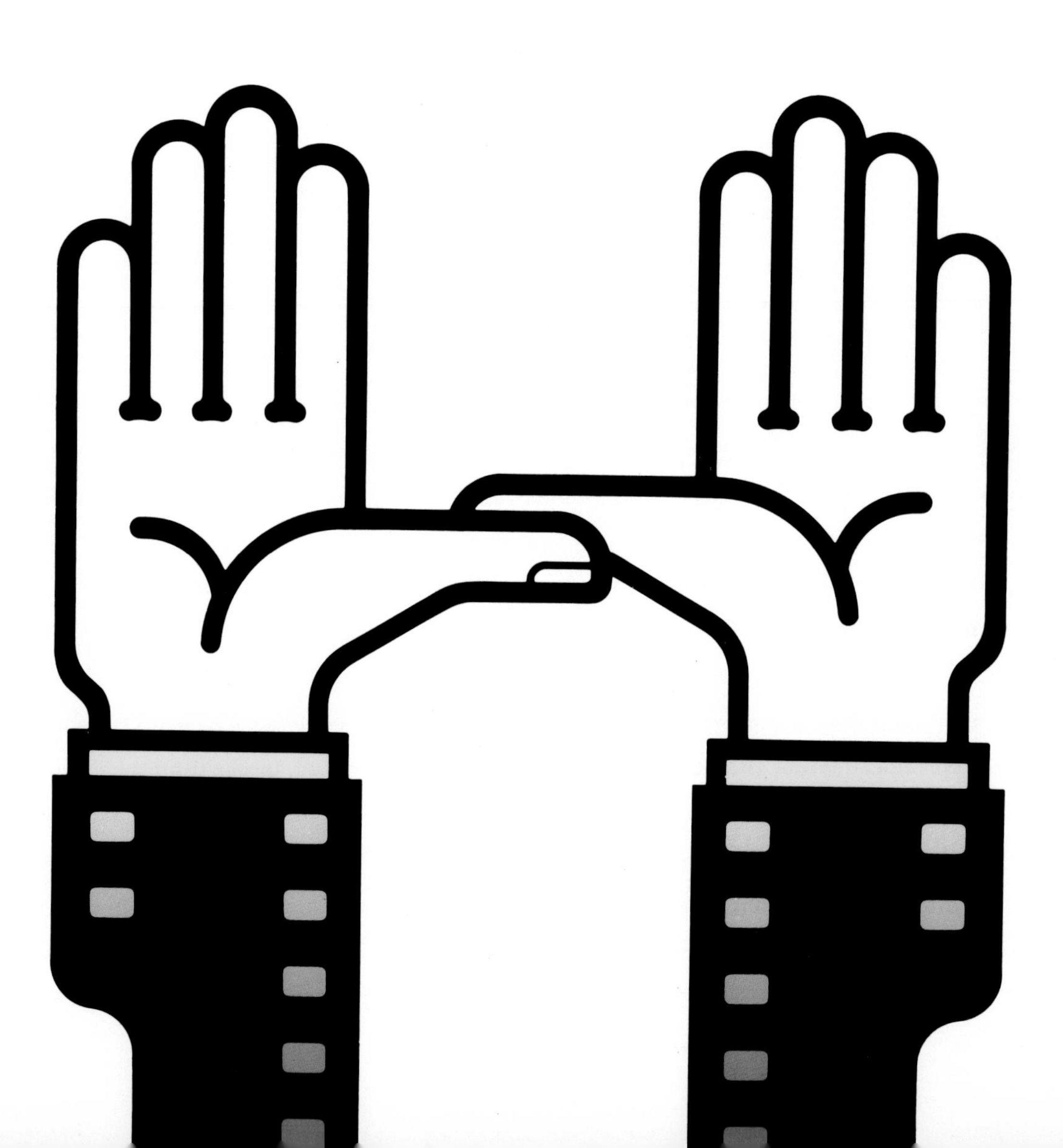

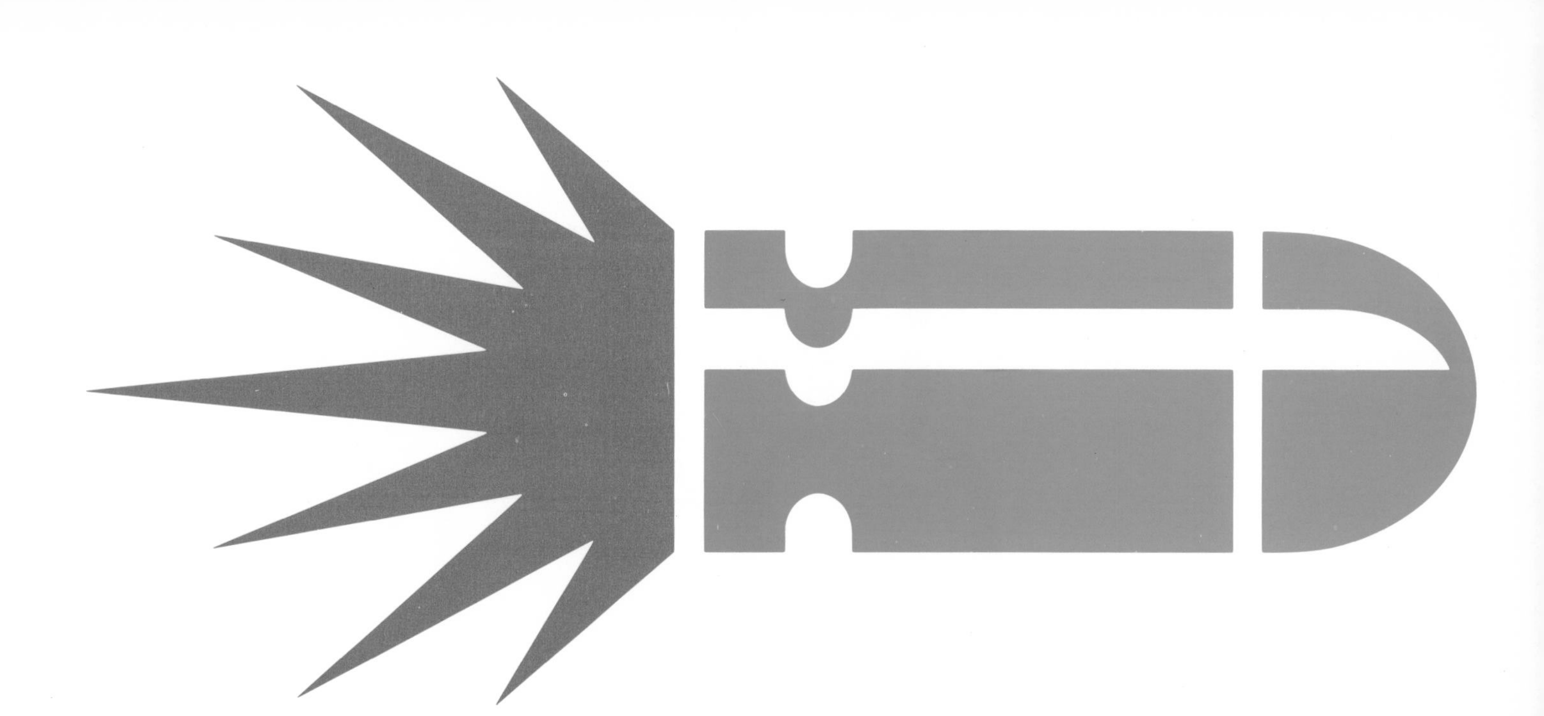

Bullet Communications

DESIGN FIRM: Bullet Communications, Chicago, Illinois

DESIGNER: Tim Scott

TGI Friday's Bartender Olympics

DESIGN FIRM: Richards, Brock, Miller, Mitchell & Associates/The Richards Group, Dallas, Texas

DESIGNER: Kenny Garrison

Mental Health Alternatives (Channeling Children's Anger Program)

DESIGN FIRM: Shapiro Design Associates, New York, New York

DESIGNER: Terri Bogaards

Manticore (Software Publishing)

DESIGN FIRM: Cook Design, Sunnyvale, California
ART DIRECTOR/ DESIGNER/ILLUSTRATOR: Mickey Cook

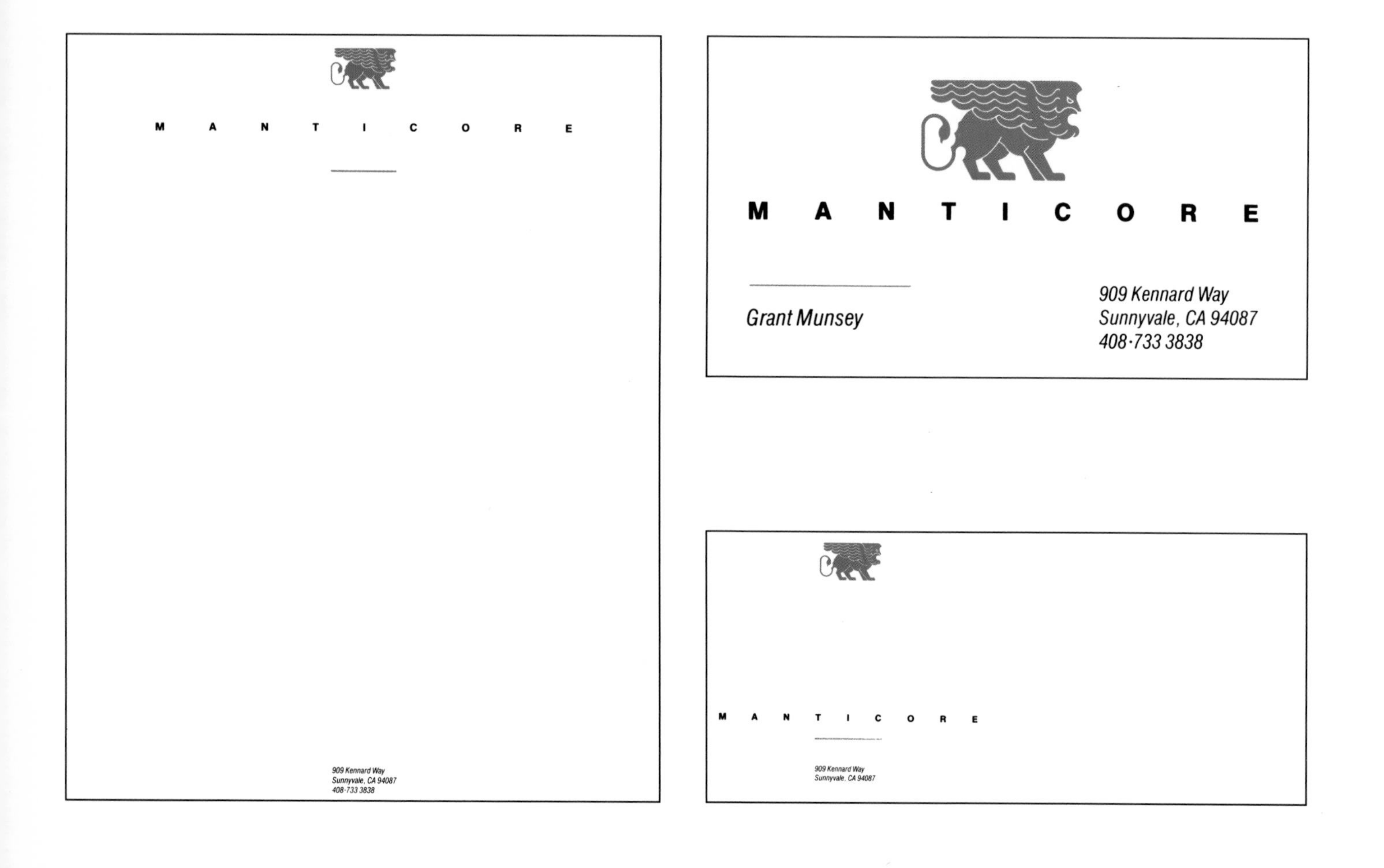

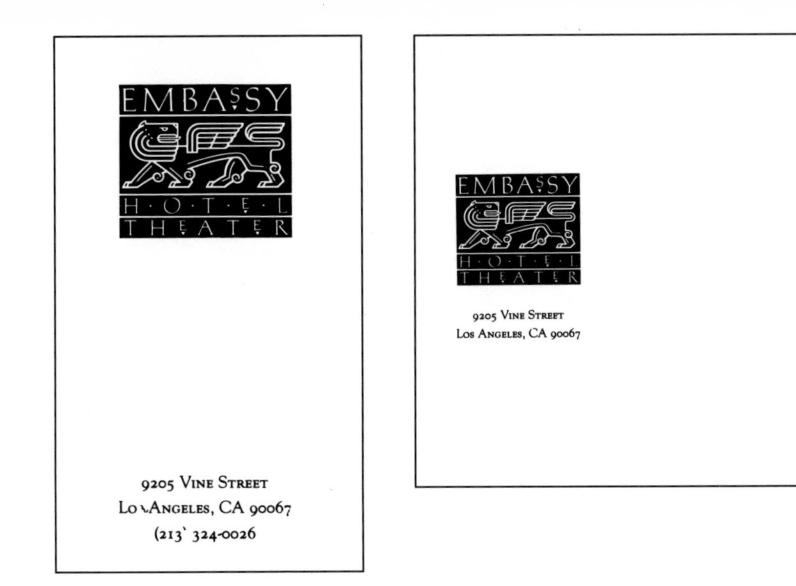

Embassy Hotel Theatre

DESIGNER/ILLUSTRATOR:

Tina Chang, Huntington Beach, California

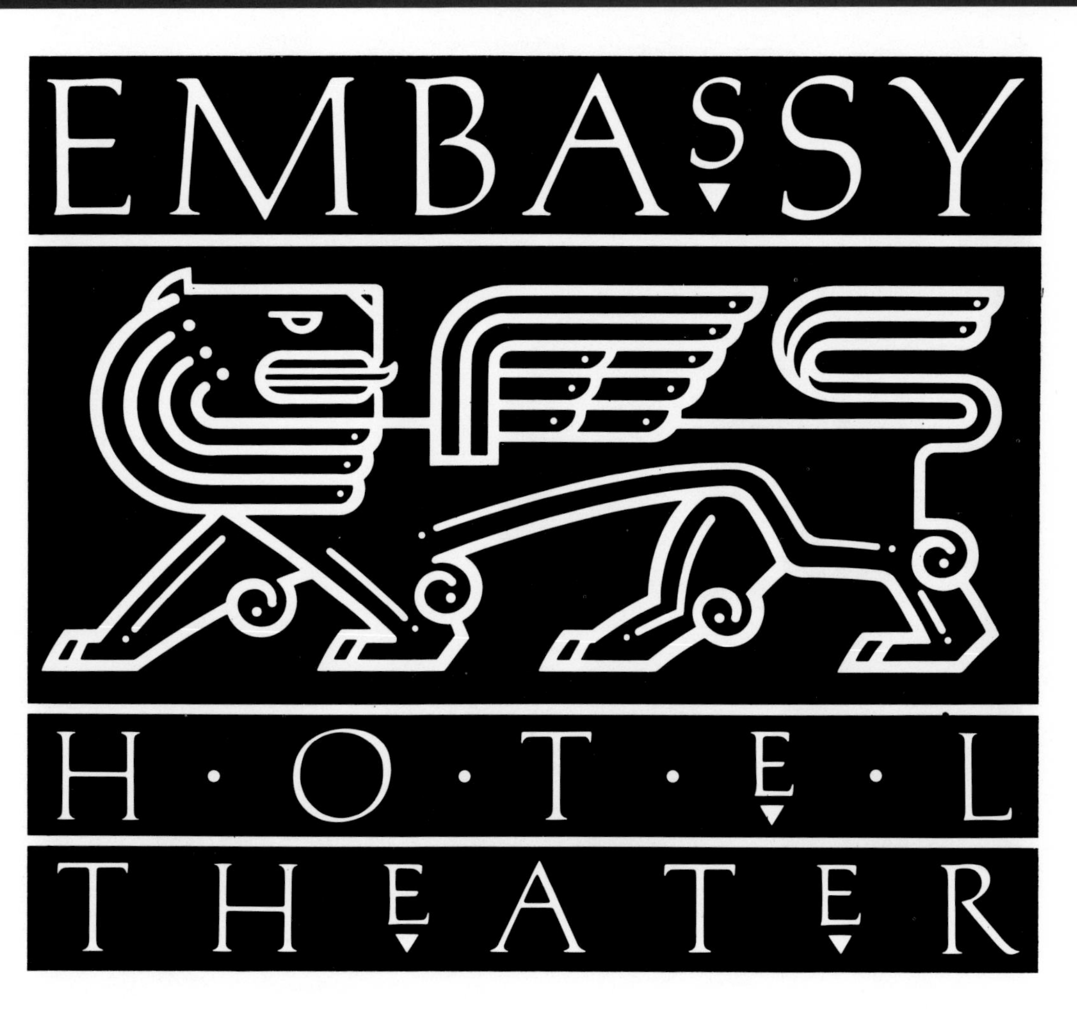

Huey Engineering

DESIGN FIRM: Loucks Atelier, Inc., Houston, Texas

ART DIRECTOR: Jay Loucks

DESIGNER: Doug Gobel

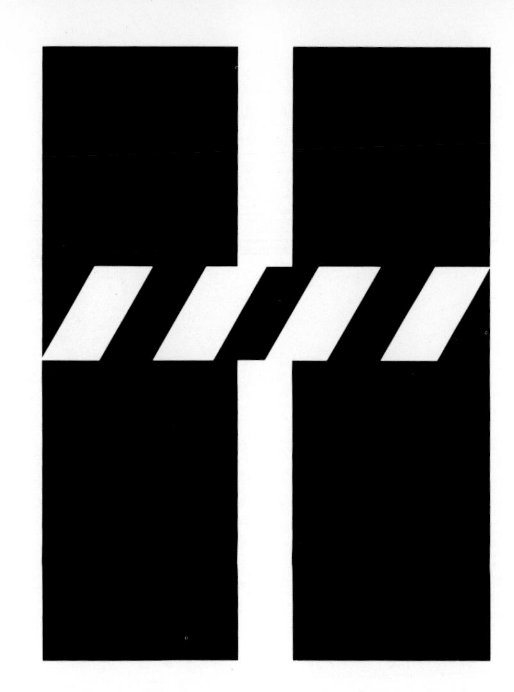

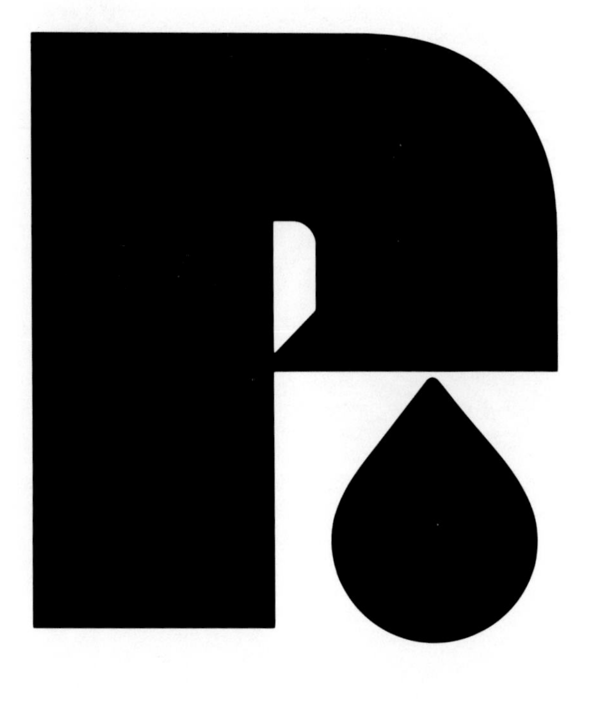

Pipeline Fuel Oil

DESIGN FIRM: Michael Gerbino Designs, New York, New York

ART DIRECTOR/ DESIGNER: Michael Gerbino

Forest McMullan Photographer

DESIGN FIRM:

Lichtenstein Marketing Communications, Rochester, New York

DESIGNER: Mark Lichtenstein

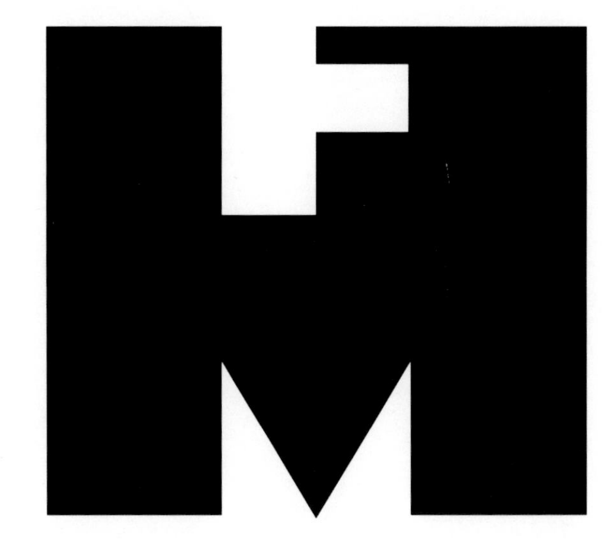

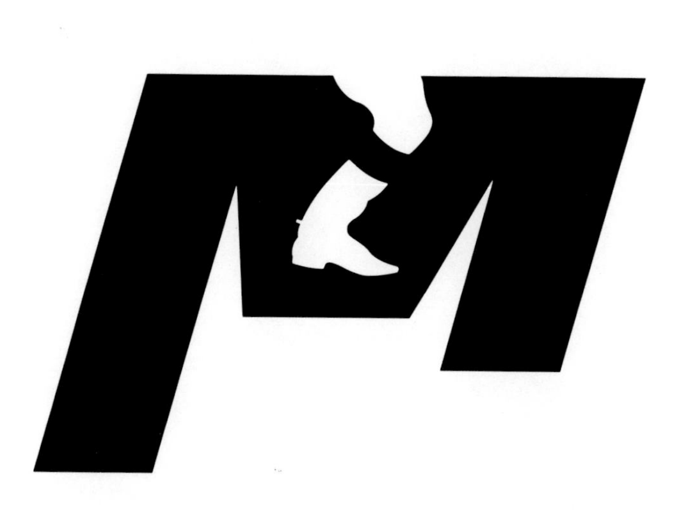

Greater Miami Valley Horse Show

DESIGN FIRM: Icon, Dayton, Ohio

ART DIRECTOR/ DESIGNER: Mark Freytag

Iaccarino and Sons (Lumber and Fine Woodworking Equipment)

DESIGN FIRM: Lapham/ Miller, Andover, Massachusetts

ART DIRECTOR: Ralph Lapham

DESIGNER: Paul Kroner

Nova Trio

DESIGN FIRM: Graphic Solutions, Key West, Florida

DESIGNER/ILLUSTRATOR: Kathi Van Aernum

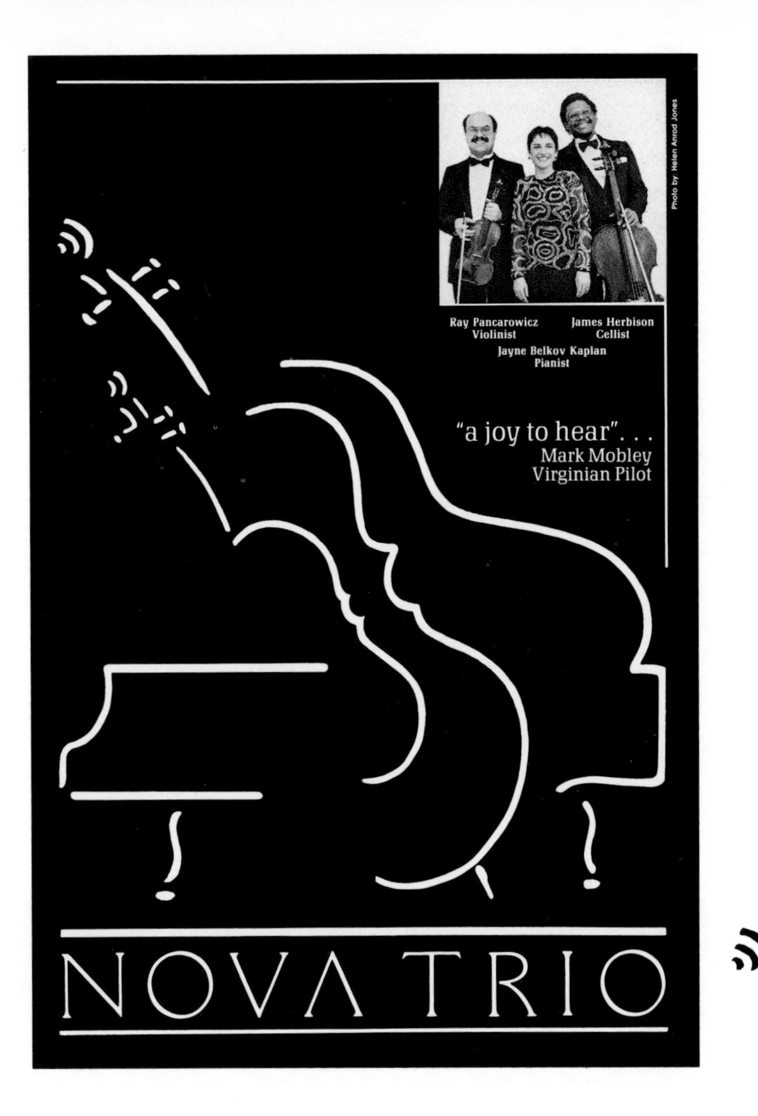

NOVA TRIO

Honolulu Zoo Studios

DESIGN FIRM: Wingard Design, Honolulu, Hawaii

DESIGNER ILLUSTRATOR: Joe Wingard

DESIGN FIRM: Yamamoto Moss, Inc., Minneapolis, Minnesota

CREATIVE DIRECTOR: Hideki Yamamoto

DESIGNER: Aimee Hucek

Southdale Pet Hospital

Dawn Cody
Professional Pet Groomer
Nationally Certified

Southdale Pet Hospital

3910 West 70th Street
Edina, Minnesota 55435
612.926.1831

Catling & Company (Advertising/Marketing)

Catling & Company
Advertising/Marketing

801 Light Street at Montgomery Baltimore, Maryland 21230 301/547-5600

Catling & Company
801 Light Street at Montgomery
Baltimore, Maryland 21230

DESIGN FIRM: Dolliver Church Design, Baltimore, Maryland

DESIGNER: Elizabeth Church Mitchell

NEWS RELEASE

DALLAS BALLET

Majestic Theatre, 1925 Elm, Suite 300, Dallas, Texas 75201, 214/744-4396

Dallas Ballet

DESIGN FIRM: Eisenberg, Inc., Dallas, Texas

ART DIRECTORS: Scott Ray, Arthur Eisenberg

DESIGNER: Scott Ray

DESIGN FIRM: Gibson Communication Group, Indianapolis, Indiana

CREATIVE DIRECTOR: Donald E. Nicholls

ART DIRECTOR: Elizabeth L. Mahoney

DESIGNER/ILLUSTRATOR: Christopher D. Hansen

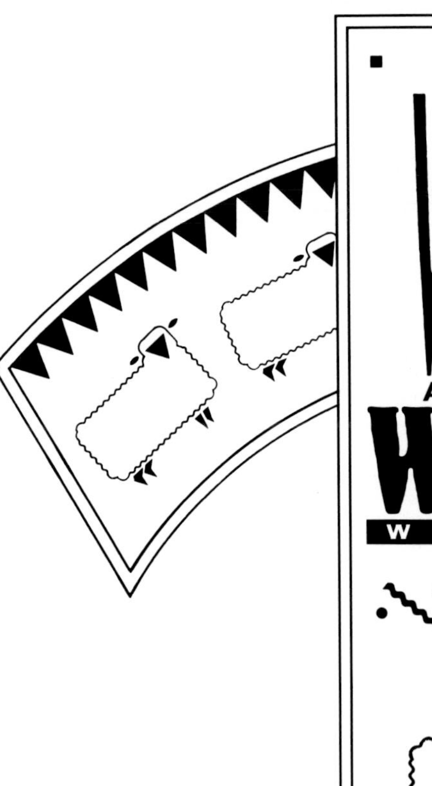

South Hills Mall (January Clearance Sale)

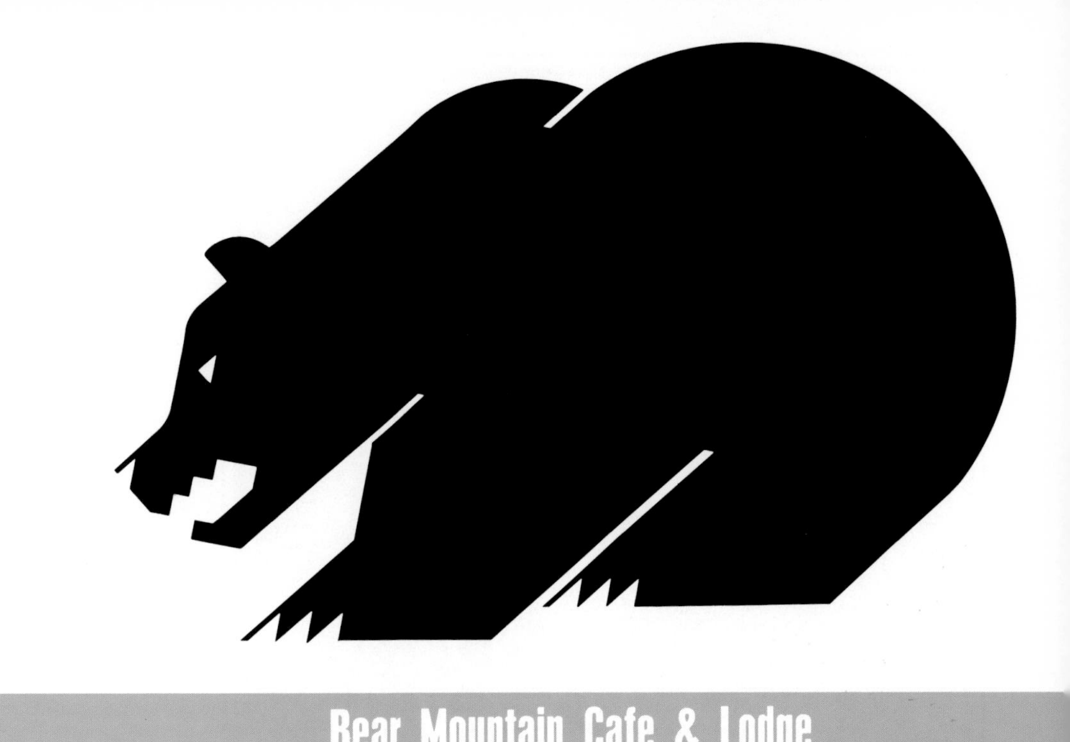

Bear Mountain Cafe & Lodge

DESIGN FIRM: Bretton Designs, Boston, Massachusetts

ART DIRECTOR: Bretton Clark

DESIGNERS: Bretton Clark, Mary Ruggieri

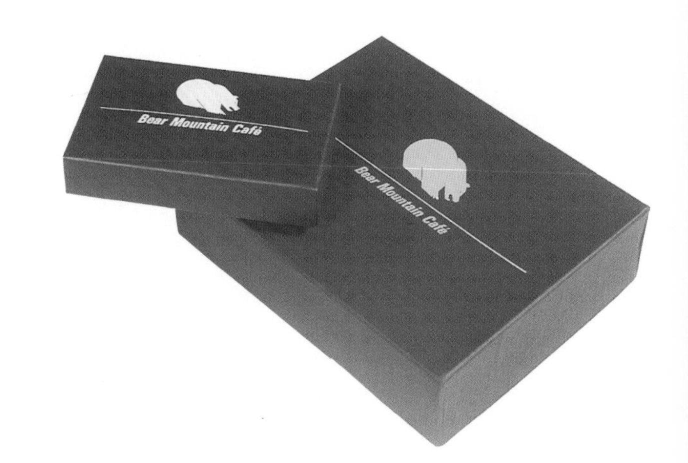

DESIGN FIRM: Muller + Company, Kansas City, Missouri
ART DIRECTOR/ DESIGNER: Patrice Eilts

Ak-Sar-Ben (Racetrack)

Academy Printers

DESIGN FIRM: Flynn

Graphic Design,

Albuquerque, New Mexico

DESIGNER: Dan Flynn

Austin Media Music

A company providing music creation and production for film and video.

DESIGNER/ILLUSTRATOR: Jim Cinq-Mars, Austin, Texas

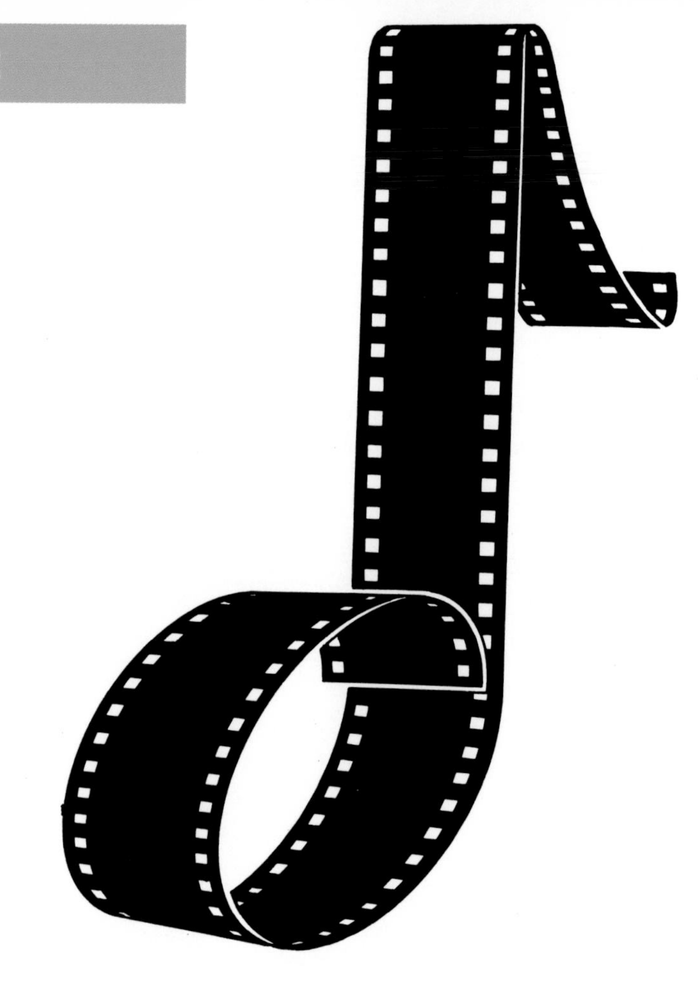

Steve Lim Productions

DESIGN FIRM: Mike Quon Design Office, Inc., New York, New York

ART DIRECTORS: Mike Quon, Steve Lim

DESIGNER: Mike Quon

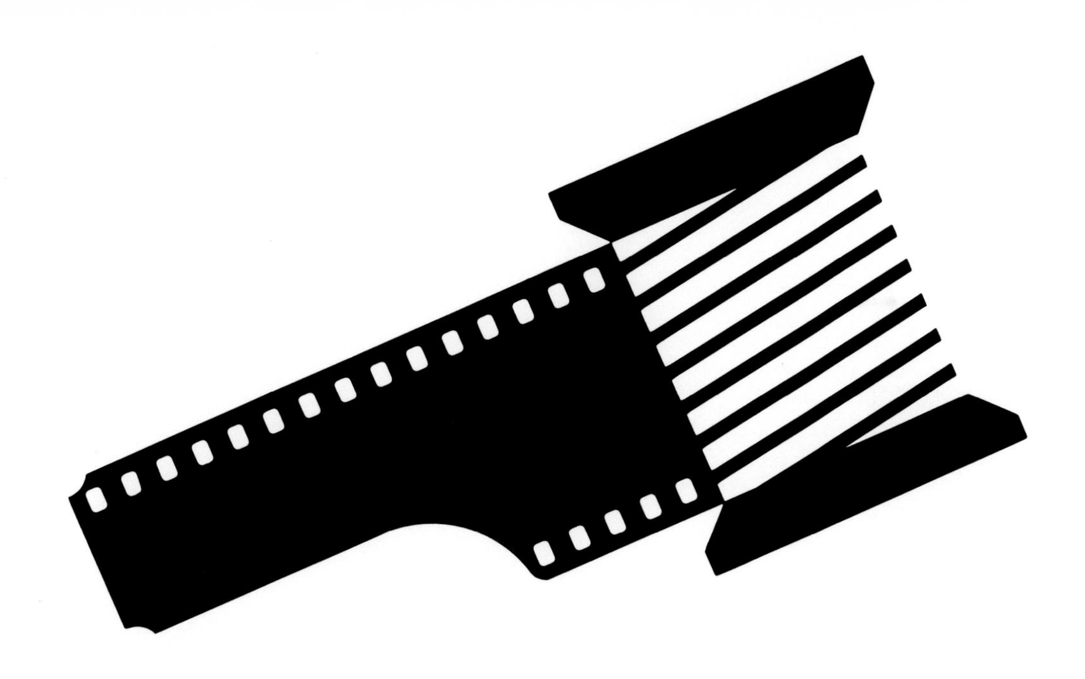

DESIGN FIRM: T&A Design, Oceanside, New York
DESIGNER: Giulio Turturro

Kevin Douglas (Fashion Photographer)

DESIGN FIRM: Poole 2, Inc., Fort Worth, Texas
ART DIRECTOR: Phillip Poole
DESIGNER/ILLUSTRATOR: Michael Connors

Hospital Movies (Movie Rentals)

DESIGN FIRM: Muller + Company, Kansas City, Missouri
ART DIRECTOR/ DESIGNER: Patrice Eilts

Day of the Dead (Folk Art Collectors)

DESIGN FIRM: Van Hayes Design, Dallas, Texas

DESIGNER/ILLUSTRATOR: Van Hayes

SILKSCREENER: Delta Graphics

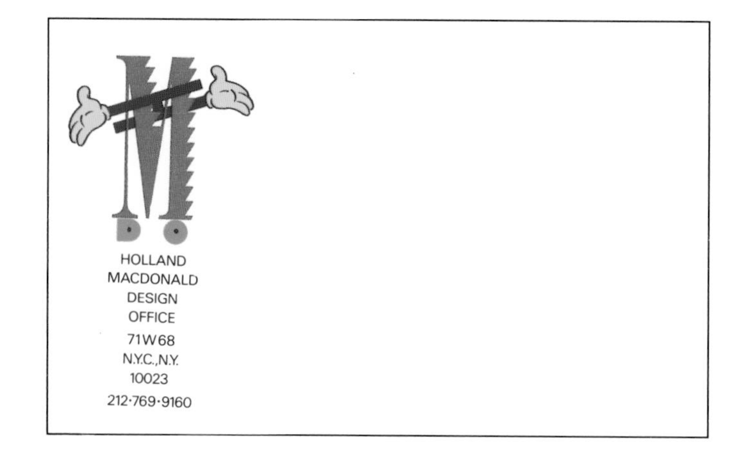

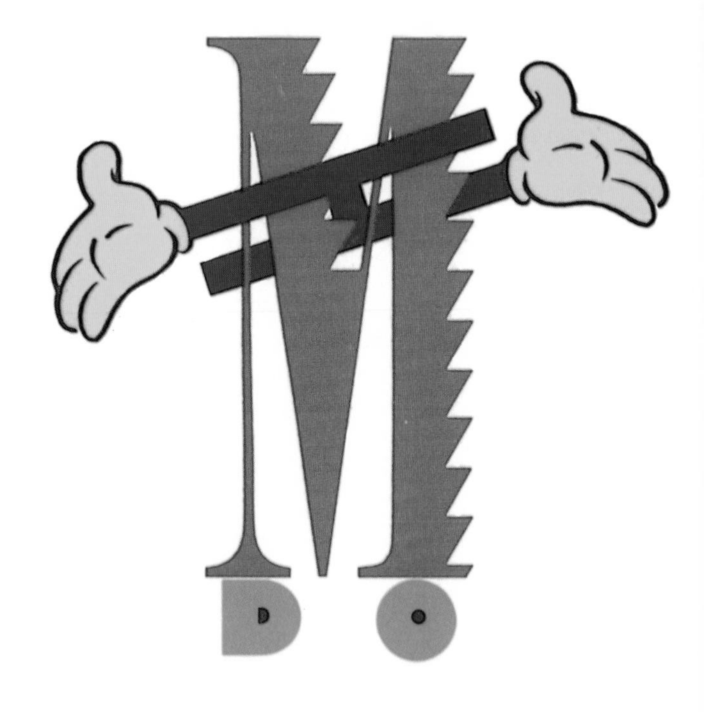

DESIGN FIRM: Holland MacDonald Design Office, New York, New York

DESIGNER: Holland MacDonald

Holland MacDonald Design Office

The Closet Organizer (Modular Closet Units)

DESIGN FIRM: Vaughn Wedeen Creative, Inc., Albuquerque, New Mexico
DESIGNER/ILLUSTRATOR: Lana Fuqua Kleinschmidt

855-C Cerrillos Road · Santa Fe, New Mexico 87501 · (505) 983-4807

Brooklyn Brewery

DESIGN FIRM: Milton Glaser, Inc., New York, New York
DESIGNER: Milton Glaser
CALLIGRAPHER: George Leavitt

DESIGN FIRM: COY Los Angeles, Culver City, California
ART DIRECTOR: John Coy
DESIGNER: Richard Atkins

UCLA College of Fine Arts

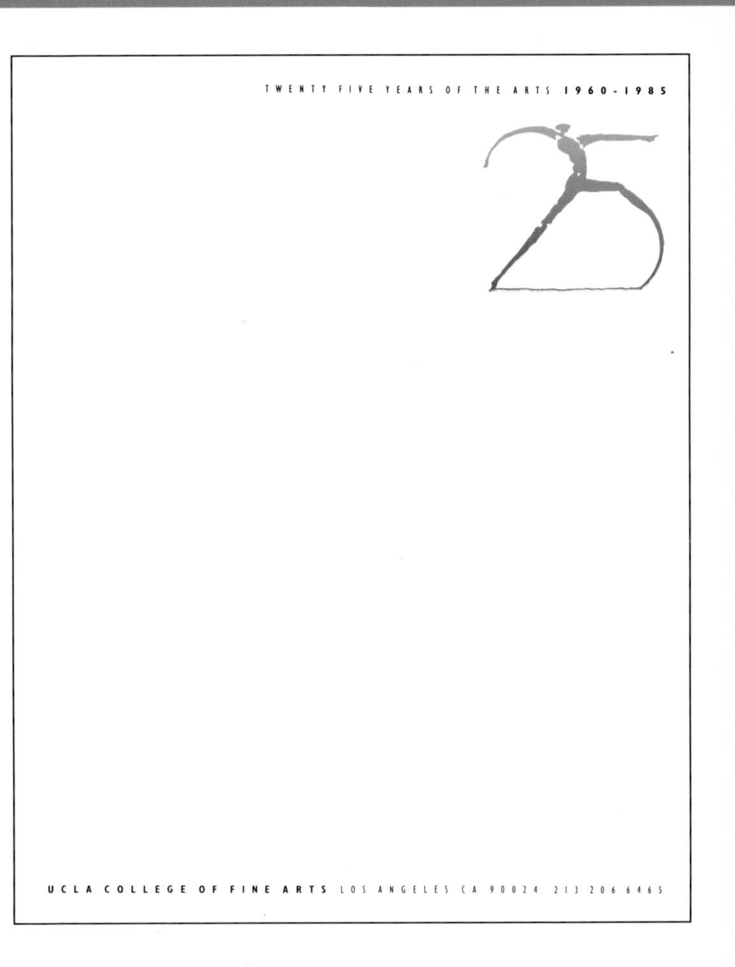

Seid Dental

DESIGN FIRM: Hegstrom Design, Campbell, California

DESIGNER: Ken Hegstrom

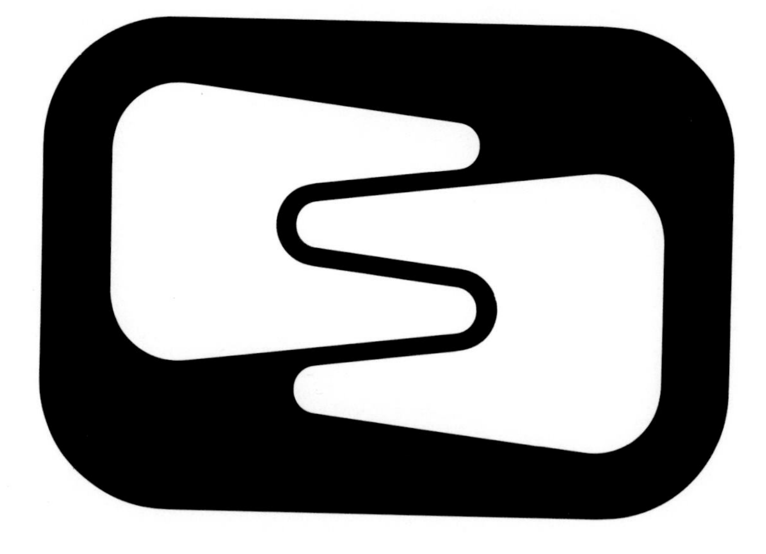

Angelico's Restaurant

A fictitious restaurant invented to teach students the principles of accounting for a small business.

DESIGN FIRM: South-Western Publishing Co., Cincinnati, Ohio

ART DIRECTOR: Debbie Gehring

DESIGNER: Craig Ramsdell

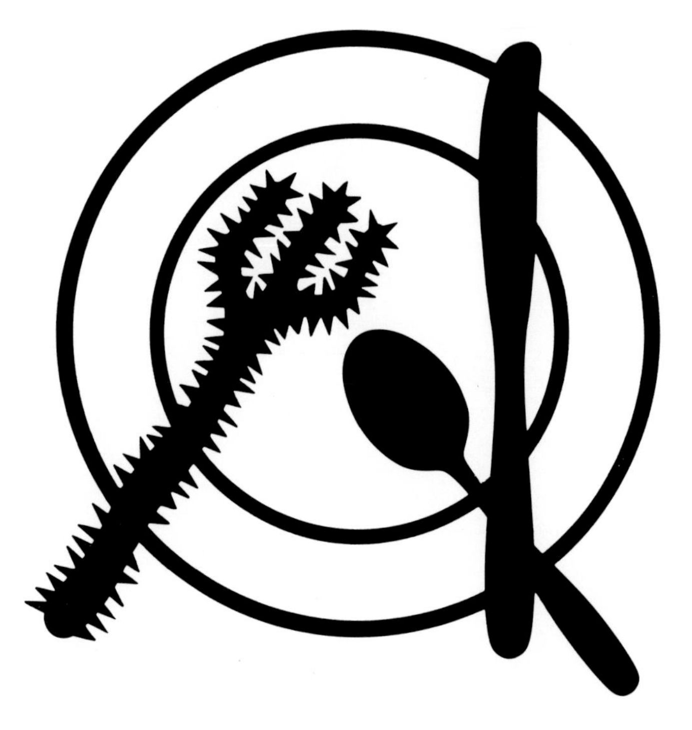

Service Writer

A computerized answering service for auto repair shops.

DESIGN FIRM: Bogusky 2, Miami, Florida

ART DIRECTOR: Alex Bogusky

DESIGNER: Bill Bogusky

ILLUSTRATOR: Tony Lampasso

Beth (A Hairdresser)

DESIGN FIRM: Hegstrom Design, San José, California

DESIGNER: John Stoneham

The Film Wave (Color Separators)

DESIGNER: Frank Pollifrone, San José, California

Marshall Drazen (Film Copywriter)

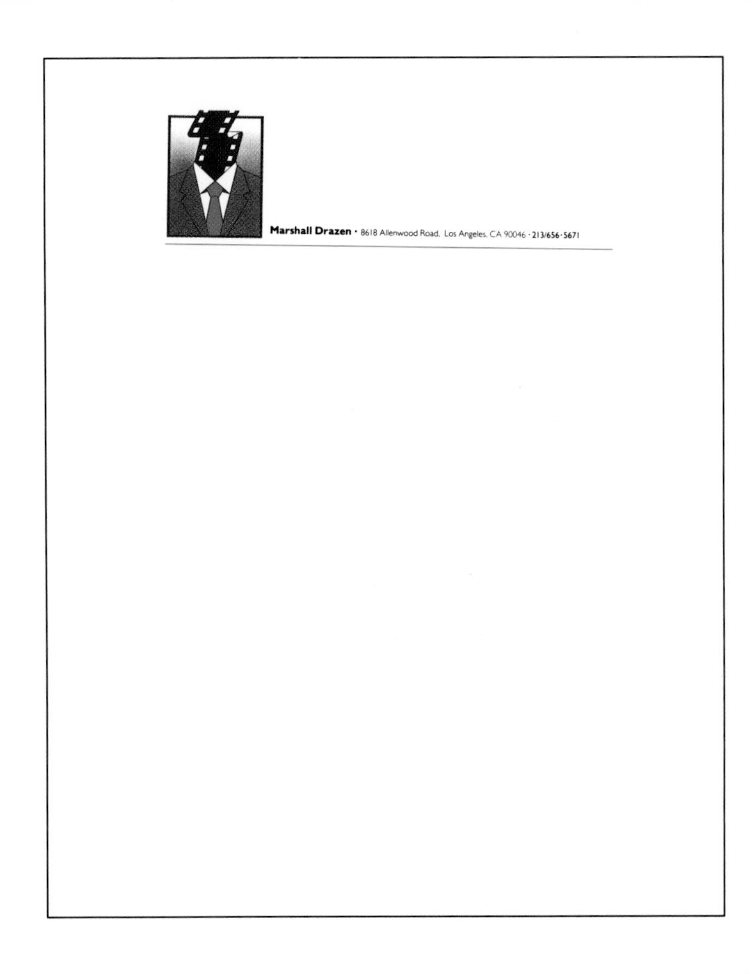

DESIGNER/ILLUSTRATOR:

John Brogna, Los Angeles, California

A non-profit organization whose main focus is to educate the public about children's issues.

DESIGN FIRM: Carlson Associates, Sacramento, California

ART DIRECTOR/ DESIGNER/ILLUSTRATOR: Nancy Lennon Hansen

TYPOGRAPHER: Ad Type Graphics

The Children's Alliance

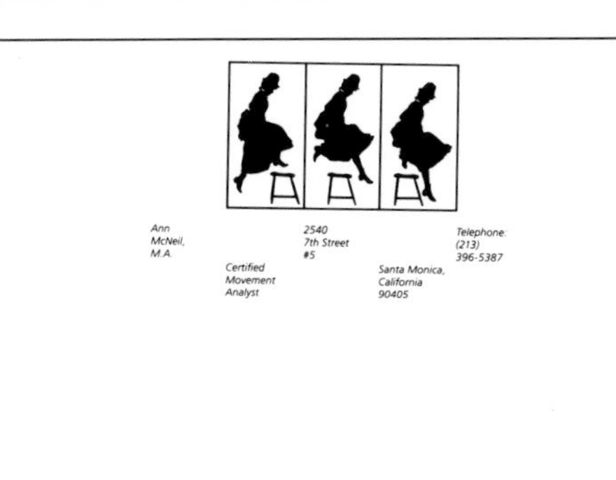

Certified Movement Analyst

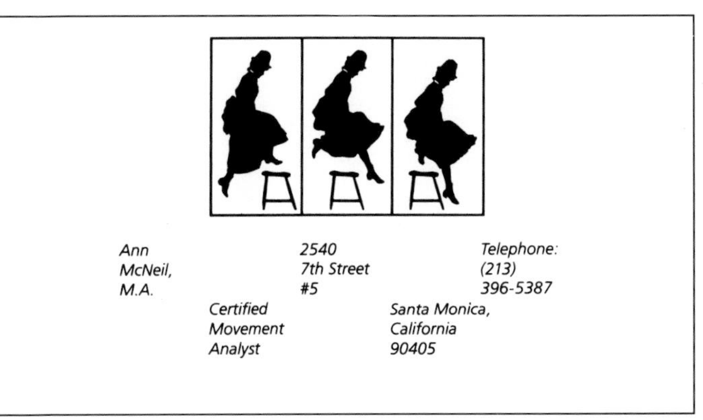

DESIGN FIRM: Alinsangan/ Doyle, Santa Monica, California

ART DIRECTORS: Susan Alinsangan, Brian Doyle

TYPOGRAPHER: Leonard Typographic

Hair Studio

DESIGN FIRM: Dunn & Rice Design, Rochester, New York

DESIGNER: John Dunn

June 12/3:00pm
LEHMAN CENTER THEATRE
Bronx Presenters Series
PRE HEAT
with Craig Harris Ensemble
and Laurie Carlos
Bedford Park Boulevard West, Bronx
Reservations & Directions:
(212) 924-0077
Tickets: $5

June 21/7:00pm
FIELDSTON SUMMER PERFORMING ARTS INSTITUTE
PERFORMANCE JAM
Fieldston Road, Riverdale
Reservations & Directions:
(212) 924-0077
Tickets: $5

August 9/6:00pm
ROBERTO CLEMENTE STATE PARK
Summer Dance Currents III
REPERTORY
West Tremont Avenue & Matthewson Road, Bronx
Information & Directions:
(212) 299-8750
Free

Urban Bush Women (Dance Group)

DESIGN FIRM: Deborah H. Payne Graphics, New York, New York

DESIGNER: Deborah H. Payne

The MotherWorks, Inc.

DESIGN FIRM: The Kottler Caldera Group, Phoenix, Arizona

DESIGNERS: David Kottler, Paul Caldera

DESIGN FIRM: Gensler and Associates/Graphics, San Francisco, California

ART DIRECTOR: John Bricker

DESIGNER: Tom Horton

Kids 'n Action

Robert Boldt Film/Video

DESIGN FIRM: Holly A. Thomas Designer, Skokie, Illinois

DESIGNER/ILLUSTRATOR: Holly A. Thomas

DESIGN FIRM: Calico Ltd., Northridge, California

DESIGNER: John Follmer

ILLUSTRATOR: Mary Burton

Hal Roach Studios

Wildlife Rehabilitation Program at Howell, Michigan, Nature Center

DESIGN FIRM: Visualeyes, Brighton, Michigan
DESIGNER/ILLUSTRATOR: Douglas Alden Peterson

Kestrel Corporation

DESIGN FIRM: Hegstrom Design, Campbell, California
ART DIRECTOR/ DESIGNER/ILLUSTRATOR: Ken Hegstrom

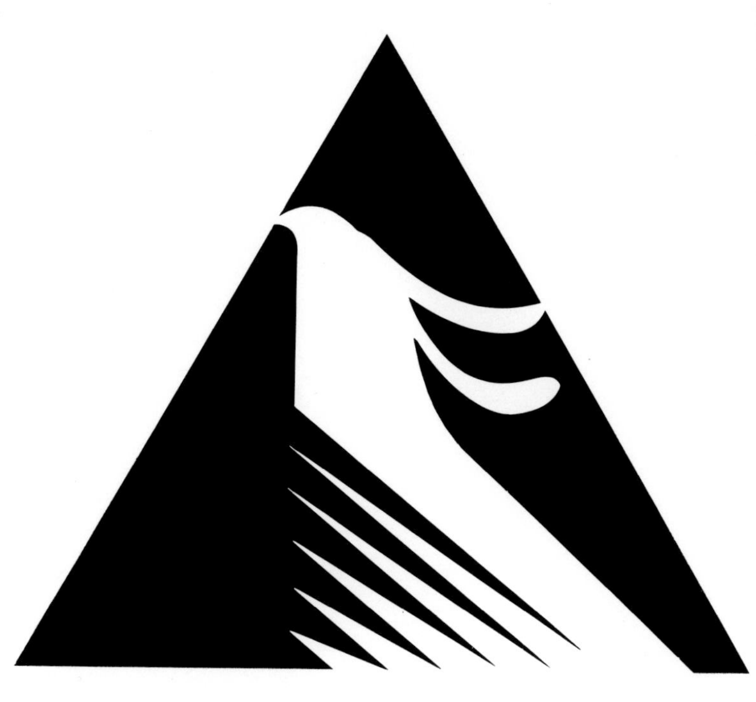

Phoenix Engineering

DESIGN FIRM: S & N Design, Manhattan, Kansas

ART DIRECTOR: Steve Lee

DESIGNER: Emil Raleigh

Southwest Inflight Music Service

DESIGN FIRM: Eisenberg Inc., Dallas, Texas

DESIGNER: Phil Waugh

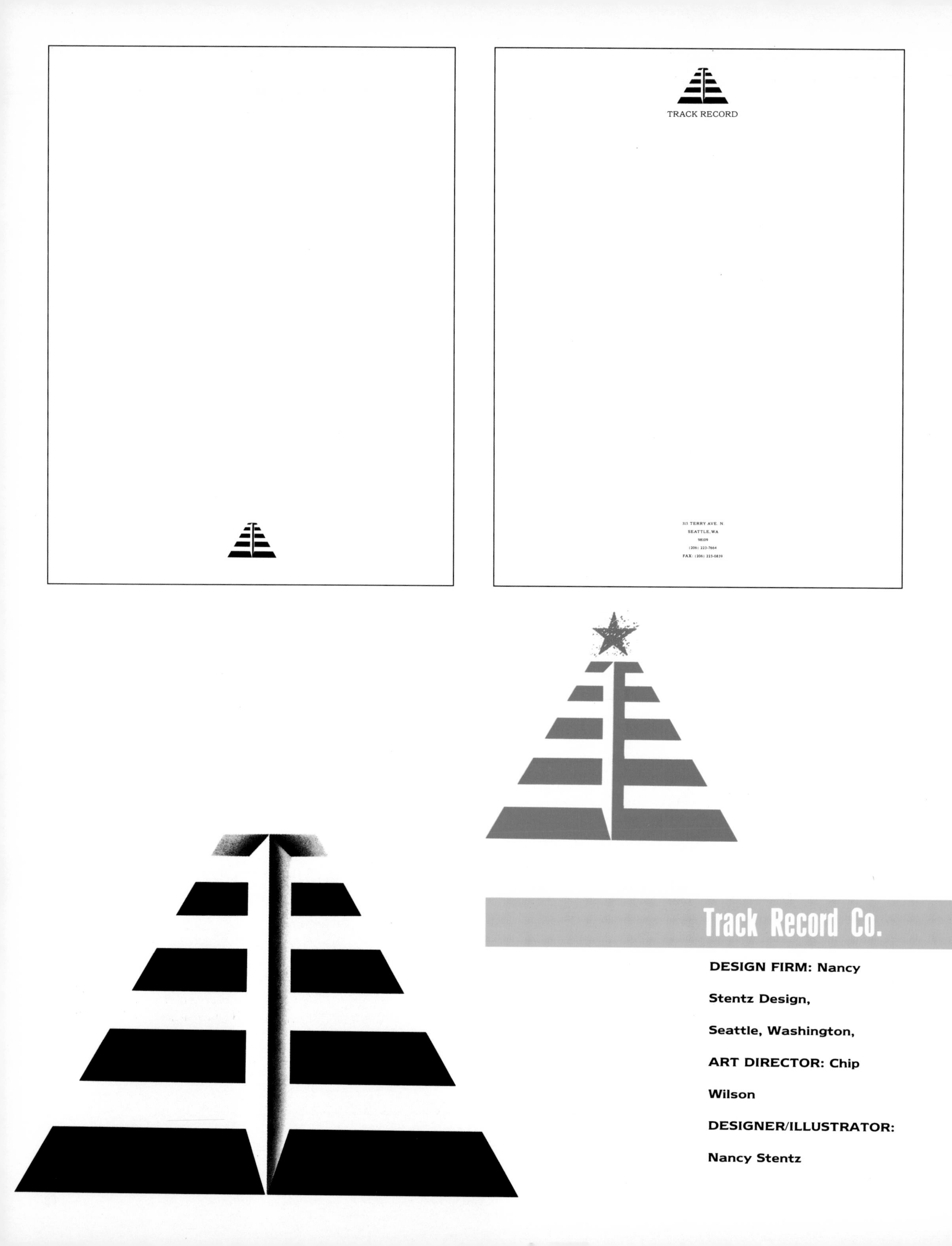

Track Record Co.

DESIGN FIRM: Nancy Stentz Design, Seattle, Washington,
ART DIRECTOR: Chip Wilson
DESIGNER/ILLUSTRATOR: Nancy Stentz

Blackstone Landing

A riverfront condominium development.

DESIGN FIRM: Design Plus, Providence, Rhode Island

ART DIRECTOR/ DESIGNER/ILLUSTRATOR: Bruce Johnson

Balanced Body (Massage Clinic)

DESIGN FIRM: The Beauchamp Group, Denver, Colorado

CREATIVE DIRECTOR: Errol Beauchamp

DESIGNER/ILLUSTRATOR Martin Miller

TYPOGRAPHER: EB Type

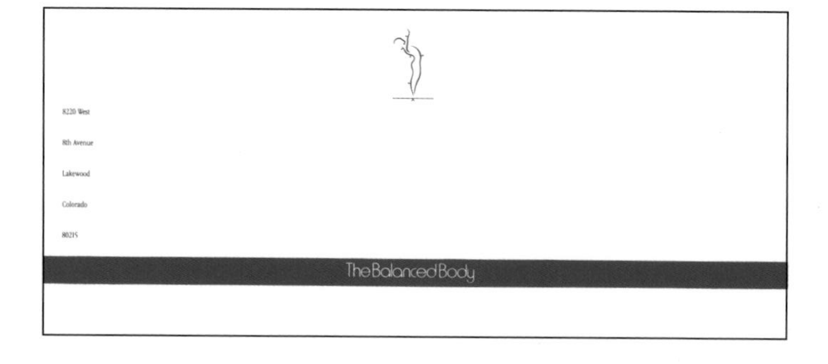

DESIGN FIRM: Pat Hansen Design, Seattle, Washington

CREATIVE DIRECTOR: Pat Hansen

DESIGNERS: Pat Hansen, Jesse Doquilo

The Well Made Bed

(206) 455-3508
990 102ND AVENUE NE
BELLEVUE, WASHINGTON 98004

THE WELL MADE BED

(206) 455-3508
990 102ND AVENUE NE
BELLEVUE, WASHINGTON 98004

THE WELL MADE BED

BOB PURE

(206) 455-3508
990 102ND AVENUE NE
BELLEVUE, WASHINGTON 98004

THE WELL MADE BED

DESIGNER: Alan J. Kegler, Buffalo, New York

Workshop on Women Playwrights

Rocky River School District

DESIGN FIRM: Petro Graphic Design Associates, Rocky River, Ohio

DESIGNER/ILLUSTRATOR: Nancy Bero Petro

DOOR DECAL DESIGNER: Helen Kariotakis

DESIGN FIRM: Janice Mataya Graphic Design, Houston, Texas
DESIGNER/ILLUSTRATOR: Janice Mataya
COPYWRITER: Donna Alexander

DESIGN FIRM: Ohio Farm Bureau, Columbus, Ohio

ART DIRECTOR/ DESIGNER: Marty Handley

Ohio Farm Bureau Federation

Universal Dance (Ballet School)

DESIGNER/ILLUSTRATOR: Michael Burke, Los Osos, California

DESIGN FIRM: Rod Brown Design, Dallas, Texas
ART DIRECTOR/ DESIGNER/ILLUSTRATOR: Rod Brown

Preston Park Bikeway

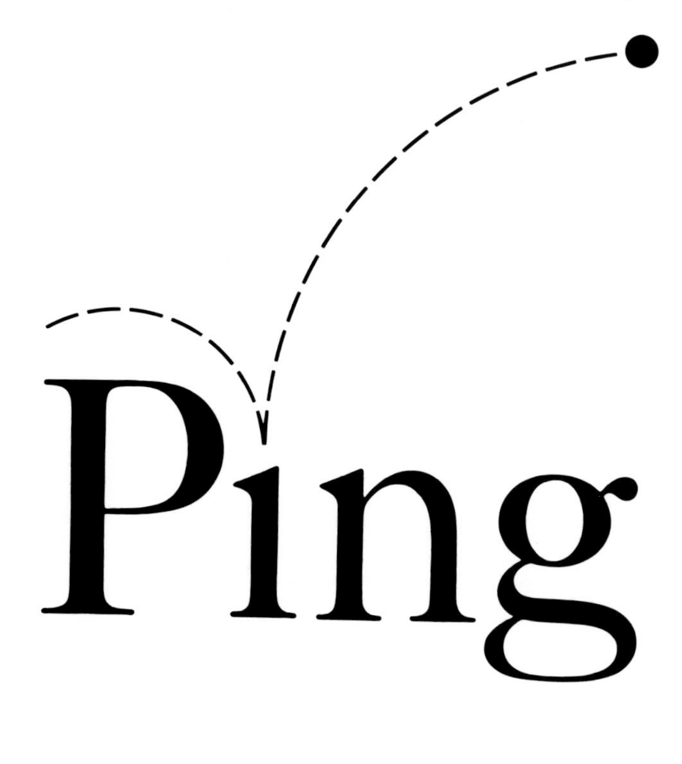

DESIGNER: Yee-Ping Cho,

Los Angeles, California

Yee-Ping Cho (Designer)

Give Peace A Dance

A 24-hour dance marathon to benefit the peace movement.

DESIGN FIRM: Art Chantry Design, Seattle, Washington

DESIGNER: Art Chantry

DESIGN FIRM: Cornerstone, Baltimore, Maryland

ART DIRECTOR/ ILLUSTRATOR: Maureen Flanigan Lindler

Victor Liberatore Associates (Interior Designers)

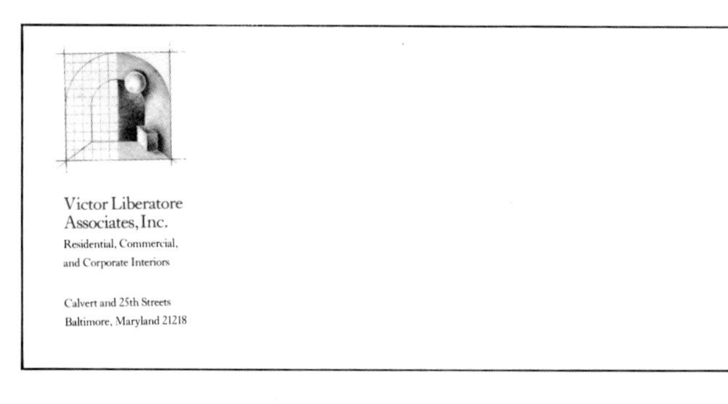

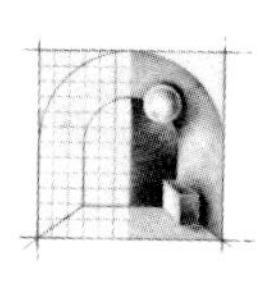

Victor Liberatore
Associates, Inc.
Residential, Commercial,
and Corporate Interiors

Calvert and 25th Streets
Baltimore, Maryland 21218
301-235-2666

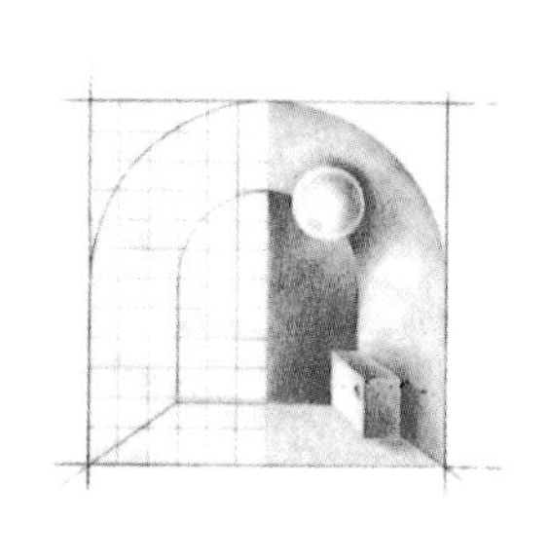

Victor Liberatore
Associates, Inc.
Residential, Commercial,
and Corporate Interiors
Calvert and 25th Streets
Baltimore, Maryland 21218
301-235-2666

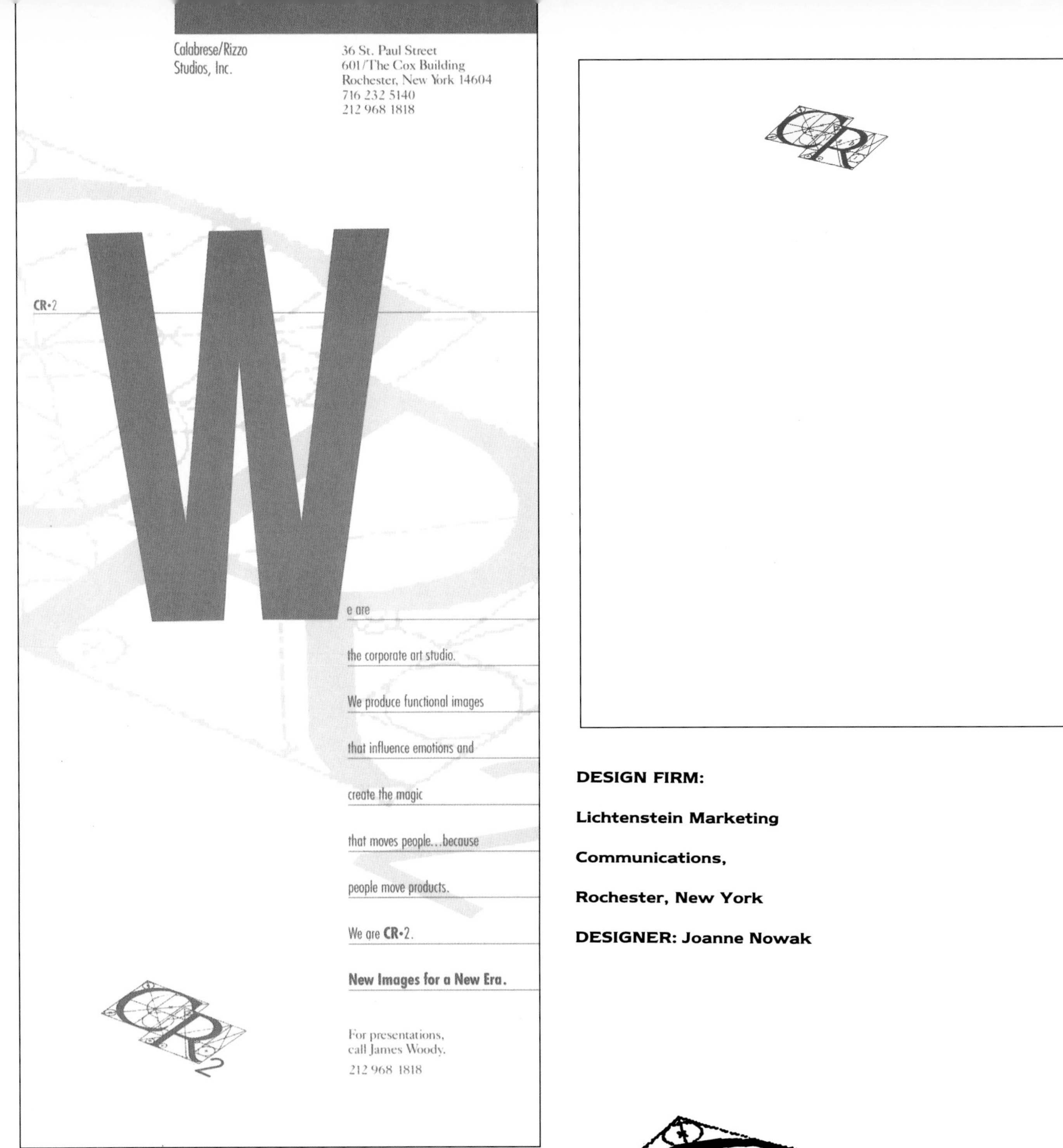

DESIGN FIRM:

Lichtenstein Marketing

Communications,

Rochester, New York

DESIGNER: Joanne Nowak

Calabrese/Rizzo Studios

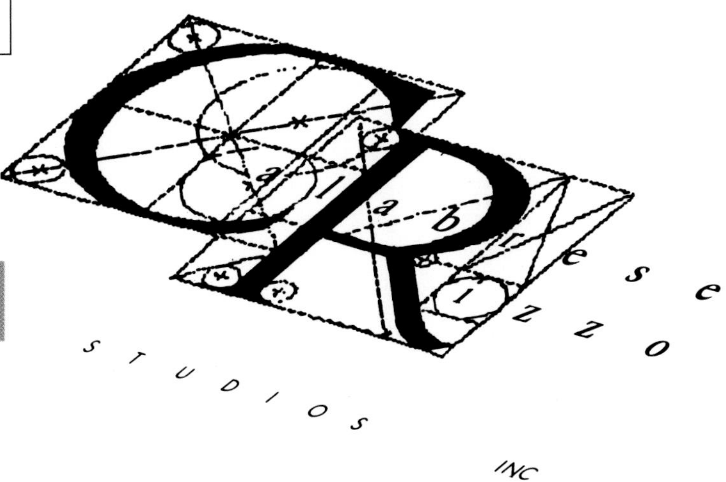

A reference service for physicians.

DESIGN FIRM: Lawson Design, Denver, Colorado

DESIGNER: Jay Lawson

AMA/NET, On-Line Computer

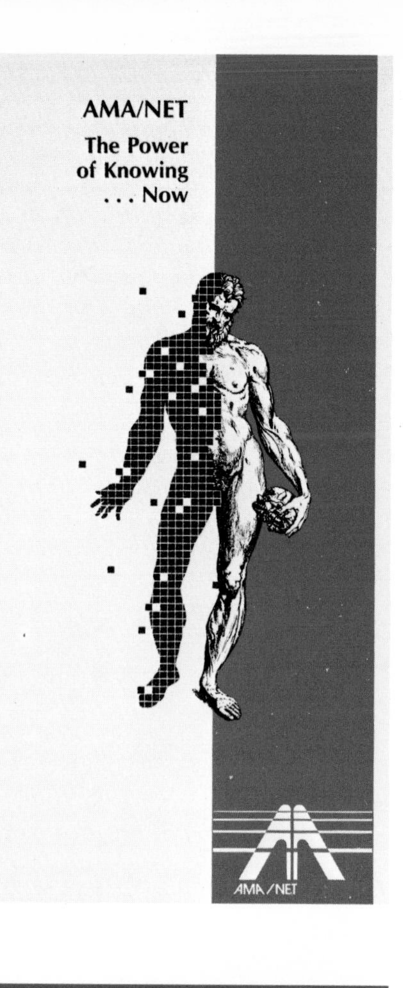

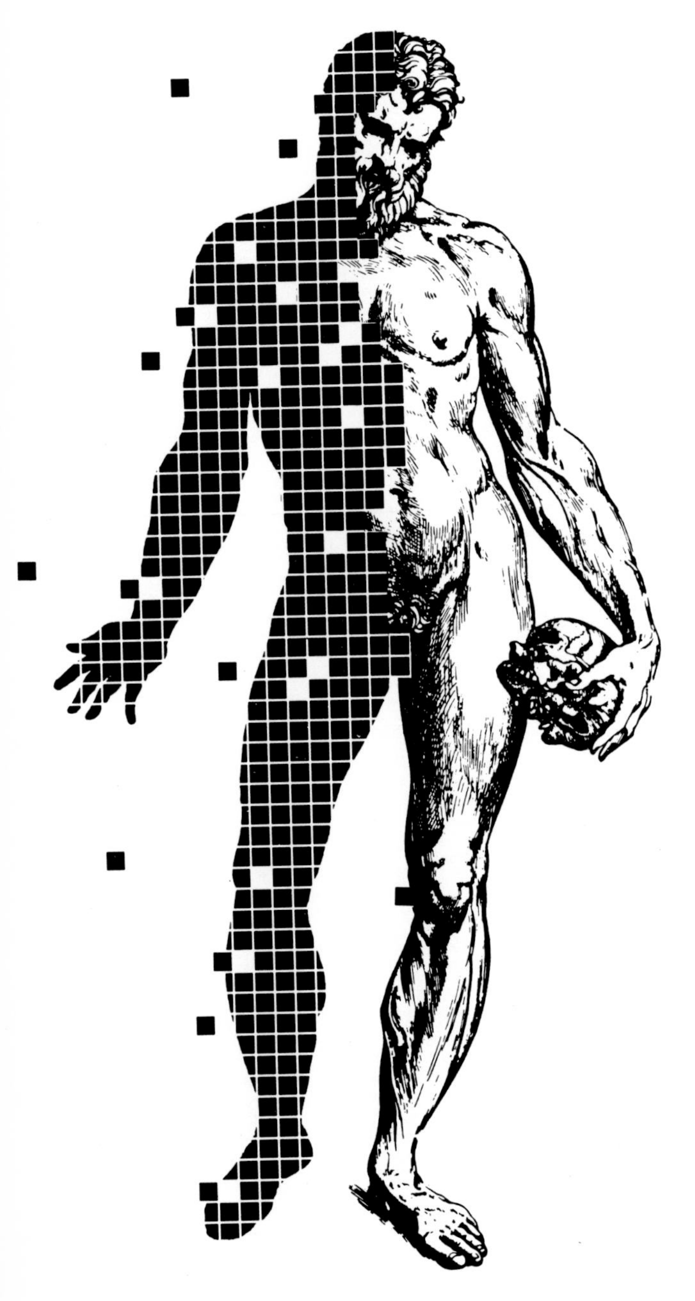

AMA/NET
Has the Answer…

Electronic Communications Designed for Professional Groups

Sponsored by the American Medical Association

On AMA/NET, your professional group can select from a broad range of electronic communication options exclusively designed to meet your memberships' needs. These options vary from a group bulletin board for posting a variety of information to rapid dissemination of personal and group communications throughout North America via electronic mail.

National Aquarium in Baltimore (5th Anniversary)

DESIGN FIRM: Shub, Dirksen, Yates & McAllister, Inc., Baltimore, Maryland

ART DIRECTOR/ DESIGNER: Daniel Shub

PHOTOGRAPHER: Robert Stockfield

Big Los Angeles Skyline Theatre

DESIGN FIRM: Shimokochi/ Reeves Design, Los Angeles, California

ART DIRECTORS: Mamoru Shimokochi, Anne Reeves

DESIGNER: Mamoru Shimokochi

International
Music
Management

6525
W. Sunset Blvd
Hollywood, CA
90028

DESIGN FIRM: Kootsillas Image Strategy and Design, South Lyon, Michigan
ART DIRECTORS: Laura Kootsillas, Linda Warren
DESIGNER: Laura Kootsillas
ILLUSTRATORS: Laura Kootsillas, Tracy DuCharme

The Creative Edge

Post Office Box 357 • Ketchum, Idaho 83340 • 208. 726. 3182

Post Office Box 357 • Ketchum, Idaho 83340

Dialogue

Partners National Health Plan patient/physician communications program.
DESIGN FIRM: Point Communications, Dallas, Texas
ART DIRECTORS: David Wesko, Anthony Fedele
DESIGNER/ILLUSTRATOR: David Wesko

DIALOGUE

Blind Mule Sports Car Racing Team

DESIGN FIRM: Abney/Huninghake Design, Louisville, Kentucky
ART DIRECTOR: Bruce Huninghake
DESIGNER: Karen Abney

Sooner Federal

DESIGN FIRM: John Harland Co., Decatur, Georgia

ART DIRECTOR/ DESIGNER: Mary Nichols DuBois

CHALKBOARD

DESIGNER: Paul Brown, Bloomington, Indiana

Chalkboard (Alumni Magazine)

Palette de Cuisine

DESIGN FIRM: S. Lynn Faier Graphic Design, Palo Alto, California

DESIGNER/ILLUSTRATOR: Lynn Faier

Symbol for restaurant's twentieth anniversary.
DESIGN FIRM: Pirtle Design, Dallas, Texas
ART DIRECTOR: Woody Pirtle
DESIGNER: Mike Schroeder

T.G.I. Friday's

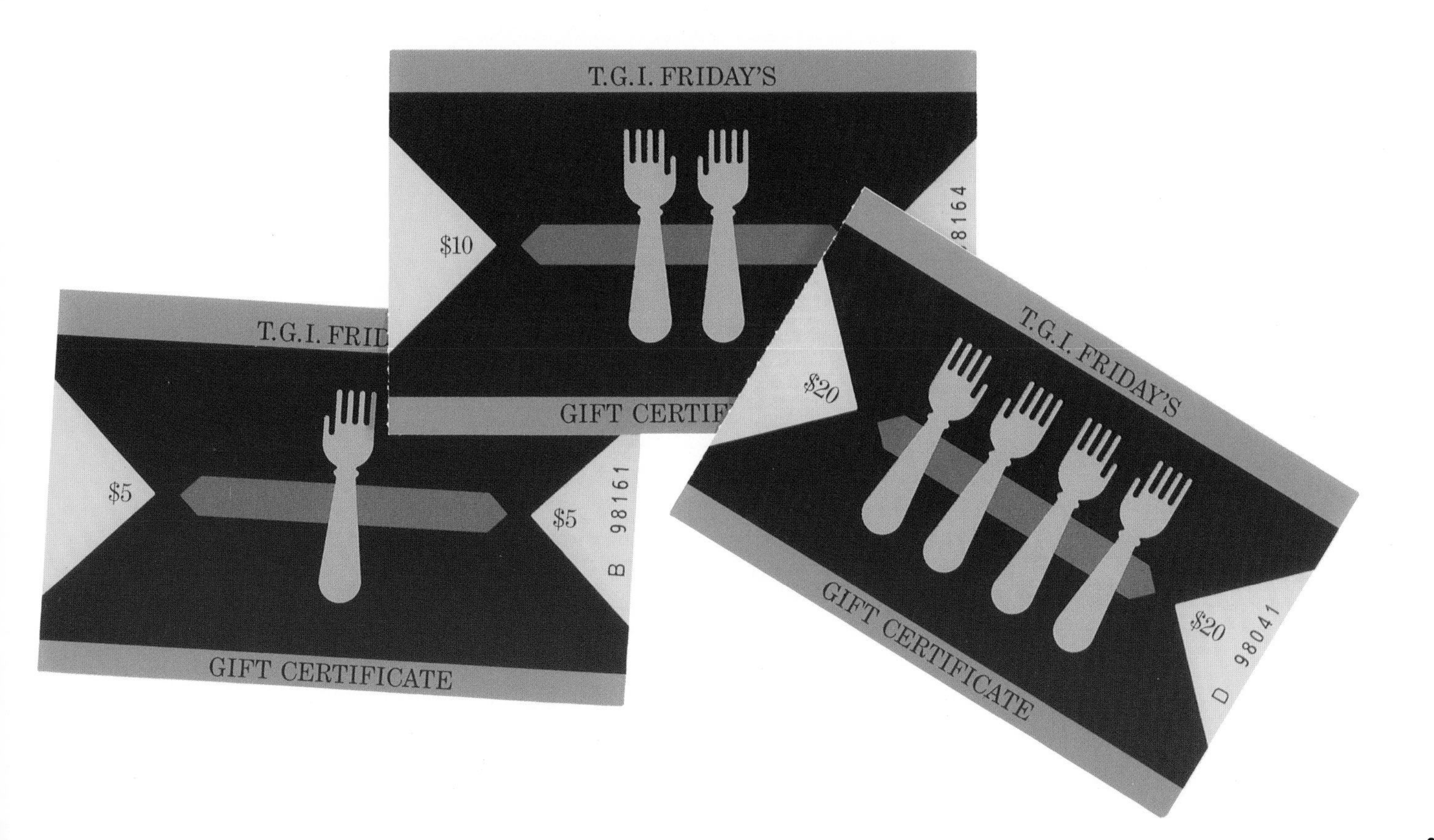

Off the Wall was released in August 1979, the same month I turned twenty-one and took control of my own affairs, and it was definitely one of the major landmarks of my life. It meant a great deal to me, because its eventual success proved beyond a shadow of a doubt that a former "child star" could mature into a recording artist with contemporary appeal. *Off the Wall* also went a step beyond the dance grooves we had cooked up. When we started the project, Quincy and I talked about how important it was to capture passion and strong feelings in a recorded performance. I still think that's what we achieved on the ballad "She's Out of My Life," and to a lesser extent on "Rock with You."

179

MJJ Products (Michael Jackson Logo)

DESIGN FIRM: Haines Wilkerson and Associates, Los Angeles, California

DESIGNER: Haines Wilkerson

MJJ PRODUCTIONS

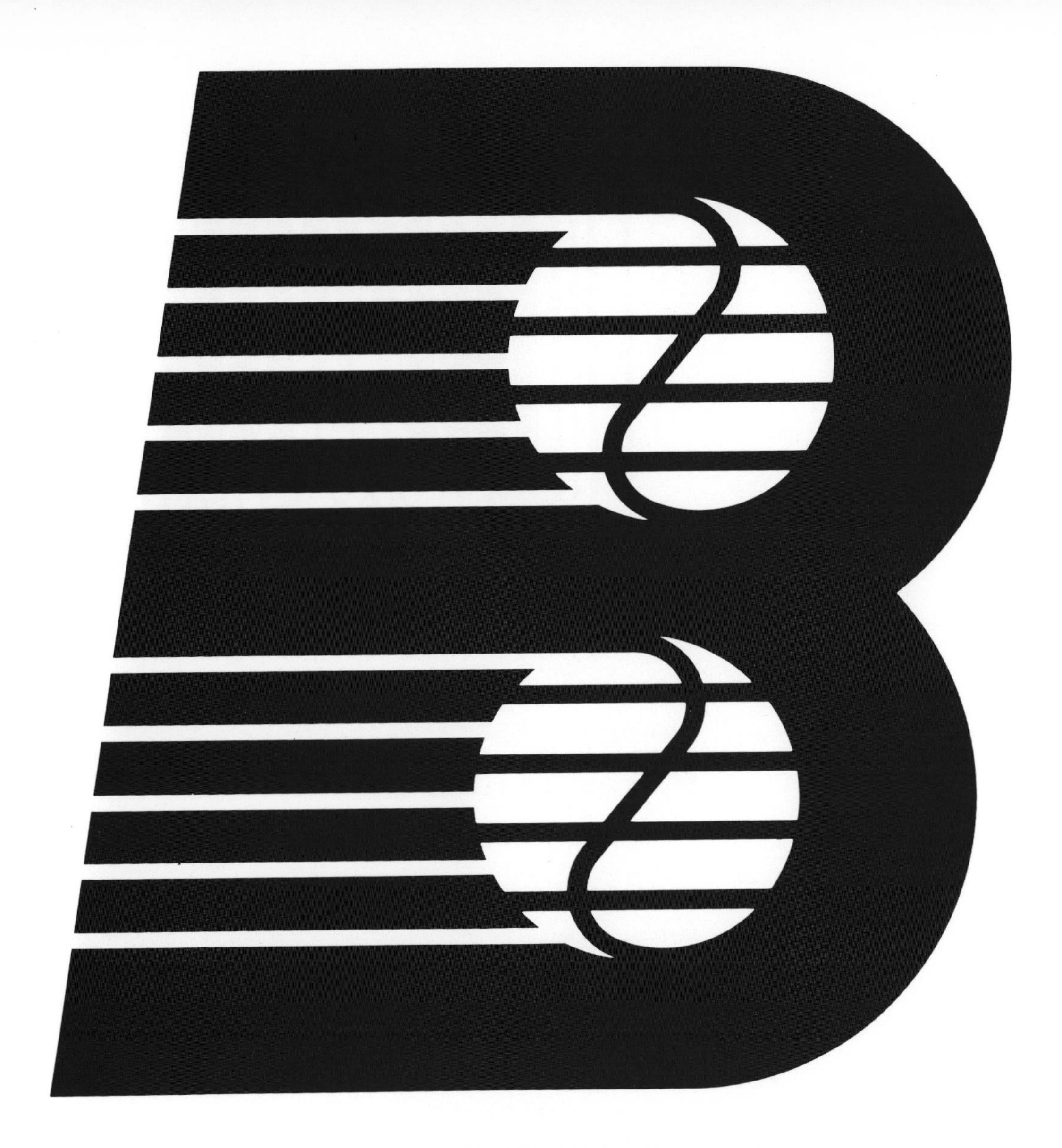

A manufacturer of baseball equipment carrying cases.
DESIGNER: Chuck Donald, Sacramento, California

Balbin

Hermsen Design Associates

DESIGN FIRM: Hermsen Design Associates, Inc., Dallas, Texas

DESIGNER/ILLUSTRATOR: Jack Hermsen

Amy Uyeki

DESIGNER/ILLUSTRATOR:

Amy Uyeki, Trinidad,

California

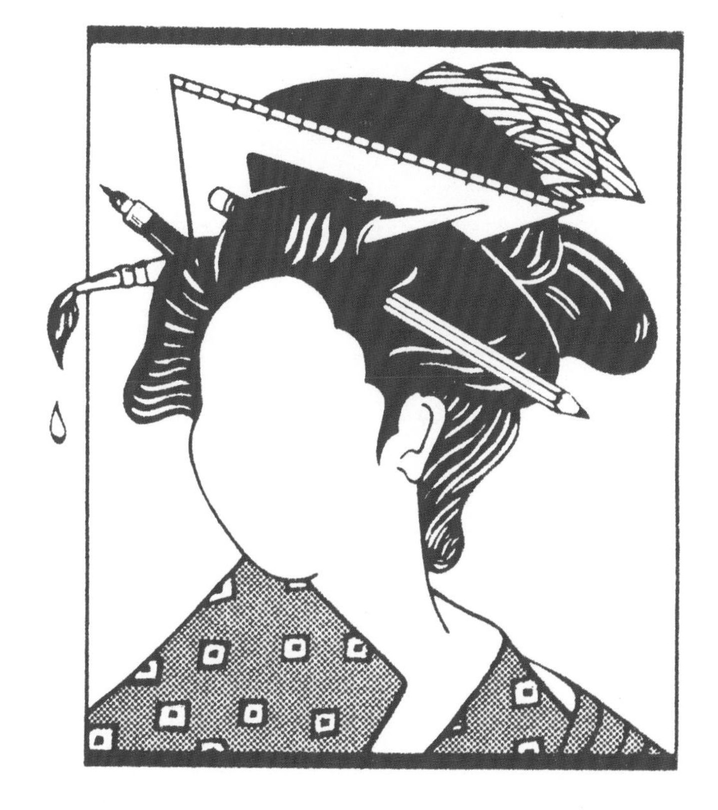

Tom Darnell Graphic Design

DESIGN FIRM: Tom Darnell Graphic Design, Austin, Texas

DESIGNER/ILLUSTRATOR: Tom Darnell

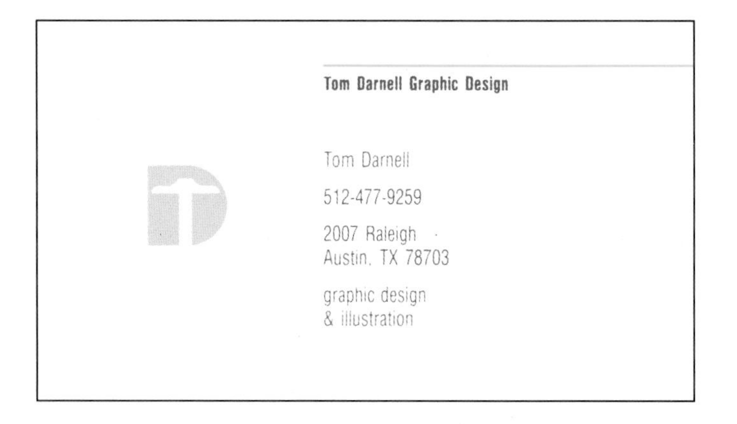

Allen
Industrial
Supply Inc.
1100 E. University
Suite 101
Tempe, AZ 85281
254-TOOL

Allen Edwards
General Manager

Allen
Industrial
Supply Inc.
1100 E. University
Suite 101
Tempe, AZ 85281

Allen Industrial Supply

DESIGN FIRM: Art Lofgreen Design, Tempe, Arizona

DESIGNER: Art Lofgreen

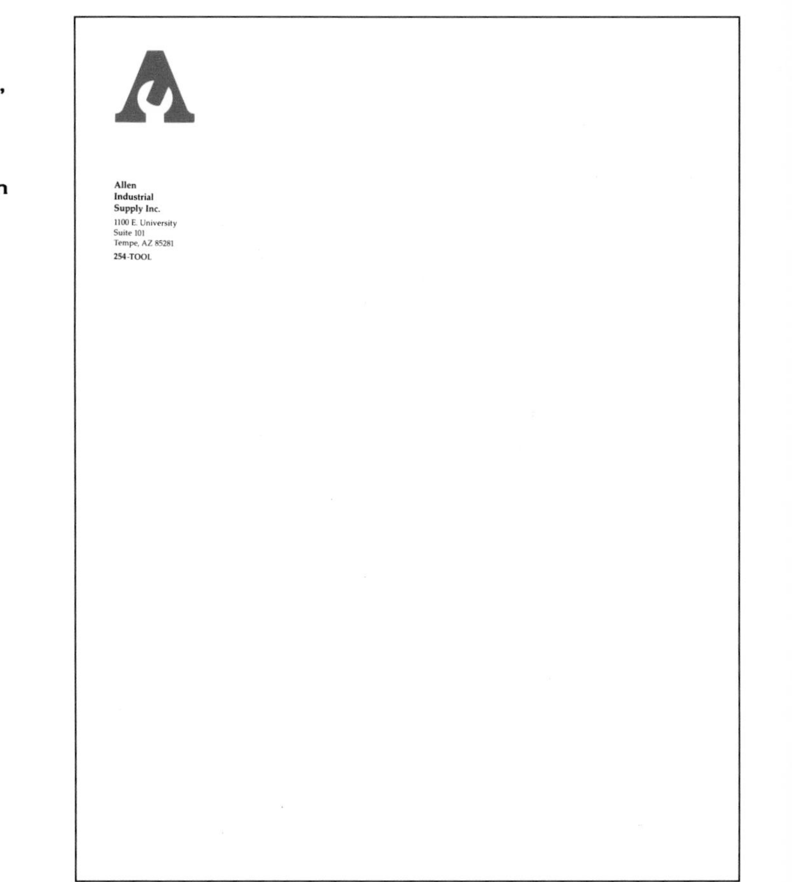

DESIGN FIRM: Heat Resistant Graphics, Cincinnati, Ohio

DESIGNER/ILLUSTRATOR: Kenn Tompos

Bovine Militia (Rock Band)

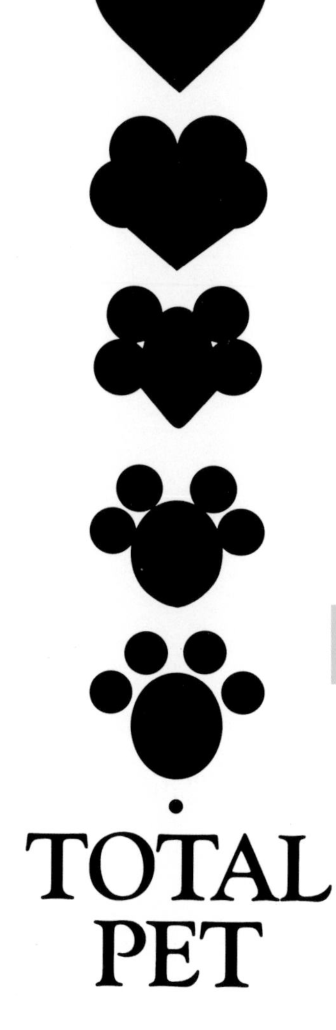

Total Pet

DESIGN FIRM: Travis Studio, Crowell, Texas

DESIGNER: Kathy White Whitley

Roadrunner Records

DESIGN FIRM: Art Lofgreen Design, Tempe, Arizona

DESIGNER: Art Lofgreen

Manhattan Laundry & Dry Cleaning

DESIGN FIRM: Eisenberg, Inc., Dallas, Texas

ART DIRECTORS: Don Arday, Arthur Eisenberg

DESIGNER/ILLUSTRATOR: Don Arday

Stroh Ranch

DESIGN FIRM: Barnhart Advertising and Public Relations, Denver, Colorado

CREATIVE DIRECTOR: David Haifleigh

ART DIRECTOR: John Murphy

DESIGNER: Richard DeOlivera

Mitch's Lawn Care and Landscaping

DESIGN FIRM: Gardner's Graphic Hands, Wichita, Kansas
ART DIRECTOR/ DESIGNER: Bill Gardner

Netek, Inc.

A fiber-optic, local area network manufacturing company.

DESIGN FIRM: Young & Laramore, Indianapolis, Indiana

DESIGNER: David Jemerson Young

ILLUSTRATOR: Wayne Watford

KAHN & COMPANY
CARPET

Quality

Color

Face Yarn

Width

Construction

Other Information

1440 Blake Street
Denver, Colorado 80202
303-573-1629
1-800-444-KAHN (5246)

KAHN & COMPANY
CARPET

Kahn & Co. Carpet

DESIGN FIRM: Primidea, Westminster, Colorado
DESIGNERS: Cynthia Vaughan (symbol), Ben Roos (signature)

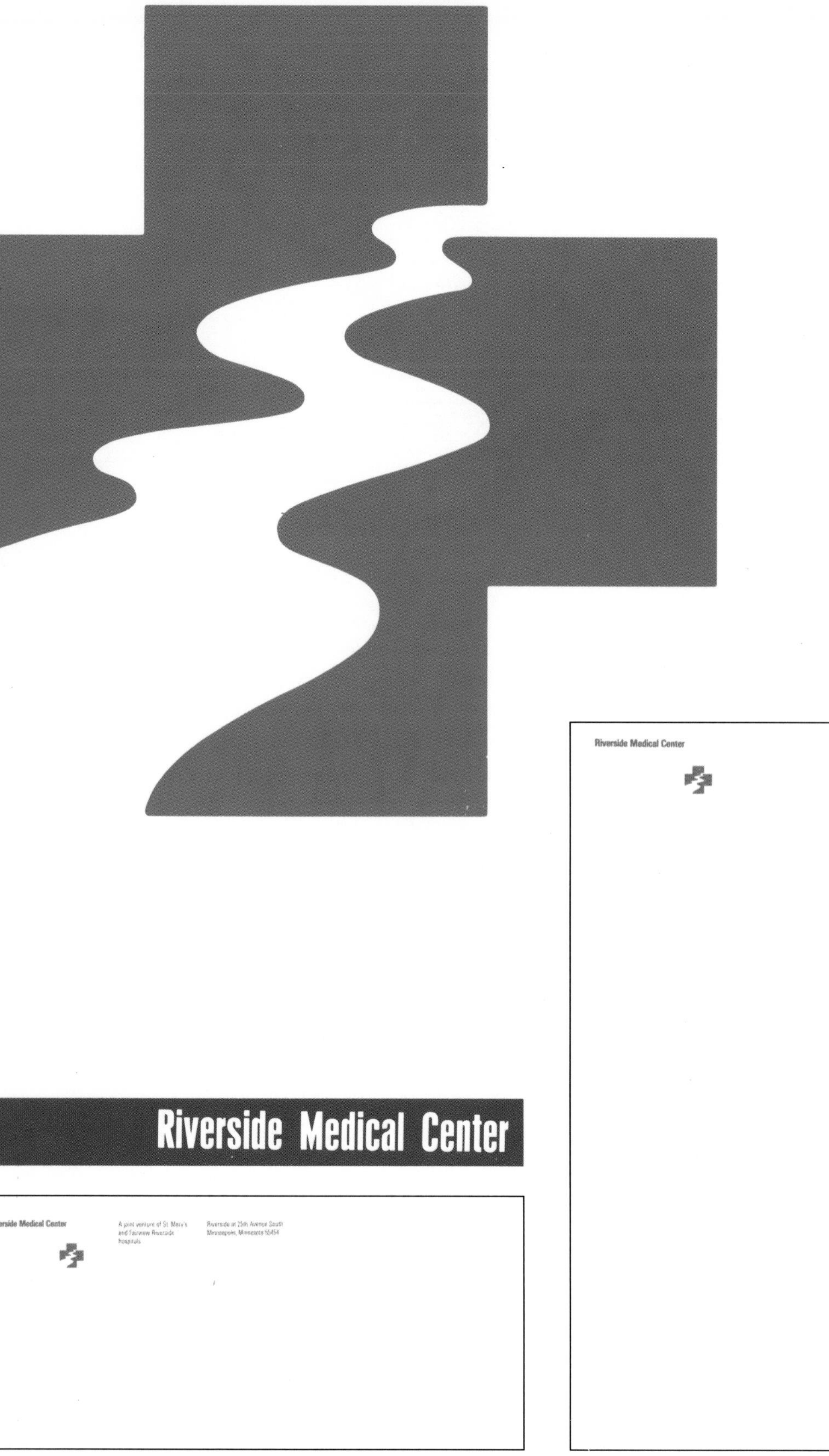

DESIGN FIRM: Design Center, Inc., Minnetonka, Minnesota

ART DIRECTOR: John Reger

DESIGNER: Dan Olsow

King Olav Dinner Committee

Logo for a dinner event during visit of Sweden's King Olav to Minneapolis. DESIGN FIRM: Rubin Cordaro Design, Minneapolis, Minnesota DESIGNER: William Homan TYPOGRAPHY: Letterworx, Inc.

DESIGN FIRM: Yonezawa Design, Seattle, Washington
DESIGNER: Glenn Yonezawa
PRODUCTION ARTIST: Eulah Sheffield

Primer Paso (Immigrant Aid Service)

PRIMER PASO INC.
• First Step Inc. •

412 South Third Street • Yakima, WA 98901
Telephone 509-453-4330

CLIENT IDENTIFICATION

PRIMER PASO INC.
• First Step Inc. •

Barry E. Stern
President

412 South Third Street
Yakima, WA 98901
Telephone 509-453-4330

Craig Record
Trainer

El Dorado Paints
521 Cottonwood Drive
Milpitas, CA 95035
(408) 434-0249
(209) 293-7865

el Dorado paints

El Dorado Paints
521 Cottonwood Drive
Milpitas, CA 95035
(408) 434-0249

el Dorado paints

El Dorado Paints (Horse Breeders)

DESIGN FIRM: Lawrence Bender & Associates, Palo Alto, California

CREATIVE DIRECTOR: Lawrence Bender

DESIGNER/ILLUSTRATOR: Margaret Hellmann Cheu

Associated Dentists

DESIGN FIRM: Jennifer Closner Design, Minneapolis, Minnesota

DESIGNER: Jennifer Closner

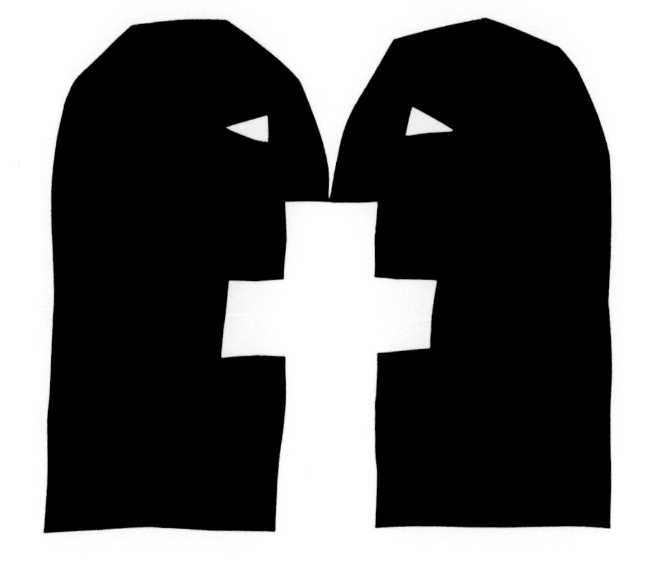

DESIGN FIRM: Richards Brock Miller Mitchell and Associates/The Richards Group, Dallas, Texas

ART DIRECTOR/ DESIGNER: Gary Templin

Marie DeCesare (Dental Hygienist)

DESIGN FIRM: Michael Gerbino Designs, New York, New York
ART DIRECTOR/ DESIGNER: Michael Gerbino

Rehabilitation Associates

DESIGN FIRM: Hawley Martin Partners, Richmond, Virginia
ART DIRECTOR/ DESIGNER: Doug Malott

Larcher
Graphic Equipment,
Inc.

5316 Carvel Road Bethesda, Maryland 20816

DESIGN FIRM: Nuttle Designs, Silver Spring, Maryland

DESIGNER: Jim Nuttle

Larcher Graphic Equipment

Galley Productions Ltd.
4033 Roberts Road
Fairfax, Virginia 22032
(703) 273-5858

INVOICE

JOB #	P.O. #	
INVOICE #	DATE	
BILLED TO		
ADDRESS		
DESCRIPTION		
BASE PRICE		
ALTERATIONS		
MINIMUM CHARGE		
RUSH CHARGE	+50%	
SUPER RUSH	+100%	
	SUB TOTAL	
	VA SALES TAX	
TERMS NET 30 DAYS	TOTAL	

Galley Productions

DESIGN FIRM: Noah's Art,

Fairfax, Virginia

DESIGNER: Dick Sisk

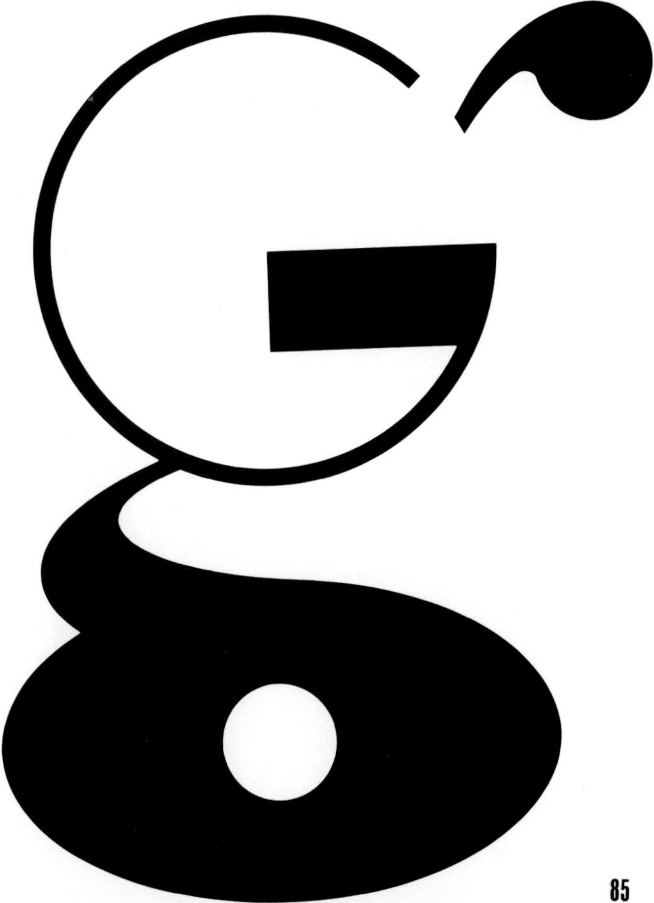

Abbeville Press

DESIGN FIRM: Abbeville Press, Inc., New York, New York

DESIGNER: James Wageman

LETTERER: Tom Carnase

488 Madison Avenue
New York, NY 10022

ABBEVILLE PRESS

ABBEVILLE PRESS

A B B E V I L L E P R E S S I N C

488 Madison Avenue
New York, NY 10022

Telephone 212 888-1969
Telex 428141 ARTAUI

Harry N. Abrams
Founder

Robert E. Abrams
President

Rice & Rice Advertising, Inc.

DESIGN FIRM: Rice & Rice Advertising, Minneapolis, Minnesota

DESIGNERS: Nancy Rice, Nick Rice

ILLUSTRATOR: Tod Apjones

THE HUNT CLUB

Chicago

The Hunt Club

DESIGN FIRM: Bobby Garland Design, Oak Park, Illinois

DESIGNER: Bobby Garland

Dan and Bev Mjolsness
Rural Route Two
Red Wing, MN 55066
612. 388. 3811

THOROUGHBRED BREEDING AND RACING

Dan and Bev Mjolsness
Rural Route Two
Red Wing, MN 55066
612. 388. 3811

Statement

Date	Description	Charges	Credit	Balance
			Total Amount Due	$

THOROUGHBRED BREEDING AND RACING

SEVEN SPRINGS
FARM

Dan and Bev Mjolsness
Rural Route Two
Red Wing, MN 55066

THOROUGHBRED BREEDING AND RACING

Seven Springs Farm

DESIGN FIRM: Gardner Graphics, Minneapolis, Minnesota

DESIGNER: Jane Flynn

ILLUSTRATOR: Jack Malloy

TYPOGRAPHER: Great Faces

Bracht Associates (Investment Services)

DESIGN FIRM: Harrison Allen Design, Houston, Texas

DESIGNER: Harrison Allen

Texas Prime Cleaners

DESIGN FIRM: Berneta Communications, Inc., Amarillo, Texas

DESIGNER: Gladys Pinkerton

TYPESETTING: Typepros

VCR Enterprises

DESIGN FIRM: Richards Brock Miller Mitchell and Associates/The Richards Group, Dallas, Texas

DESIGNER: Robert Forsbach

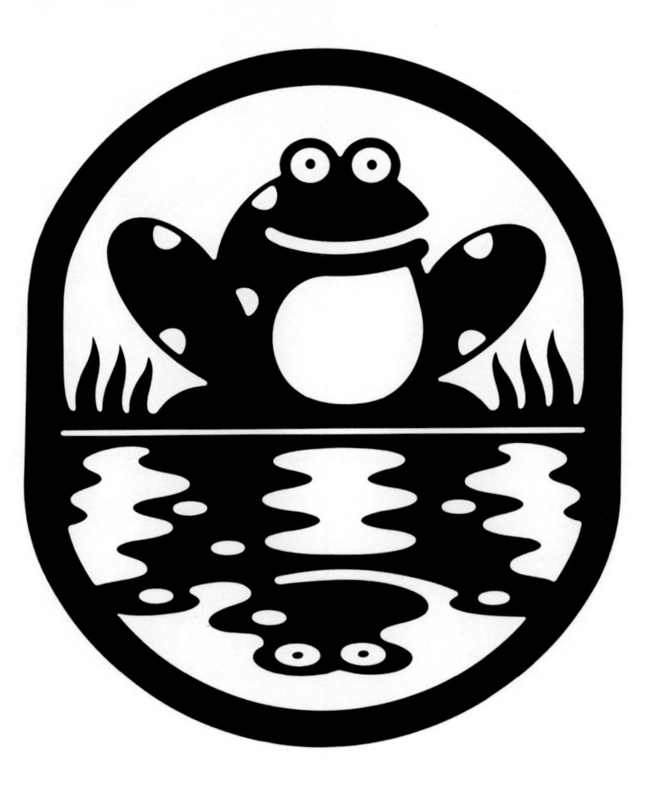

DESIGN FIRM: Kelliher Design, Kansas City, Missouri

DESIGNER: Kevin Kelliher

Electric Pig Café

City of Coon Rapids

DESIGN FIRM: Duffy Design Group, Minneapolis, Minnesota

ART DIRECTOR/ DESIGNER: Charles S. Anderson

ILLUSTRATORS: Charles S. Anderson, Lynn Schulte

Down to Earth (Natural Foods & Garden Supplies)

DESIGN FIRM: Scribble, Washington, D.C.

ART DIRECTOR/ DESIGNER: Gayle Monkkonen

Architectural Book Center

DESIGN FIRM: Young Martin Massey, Atlanta, Georgia

DESIGNER/ILLUSTRATOR: Ed Young

Architectural Book Center
Colony Square
Retail Mall/Mall Level
1197 Peachtree Street, N.E.
Atlanta, GA 30361
404/873-3207

Keegan/Troup Construction

DESIGN FIRM: Weller Institute for Cure of Design, Park City, Utah

DESIGNER/ILLUSTRATOR: Don Weller

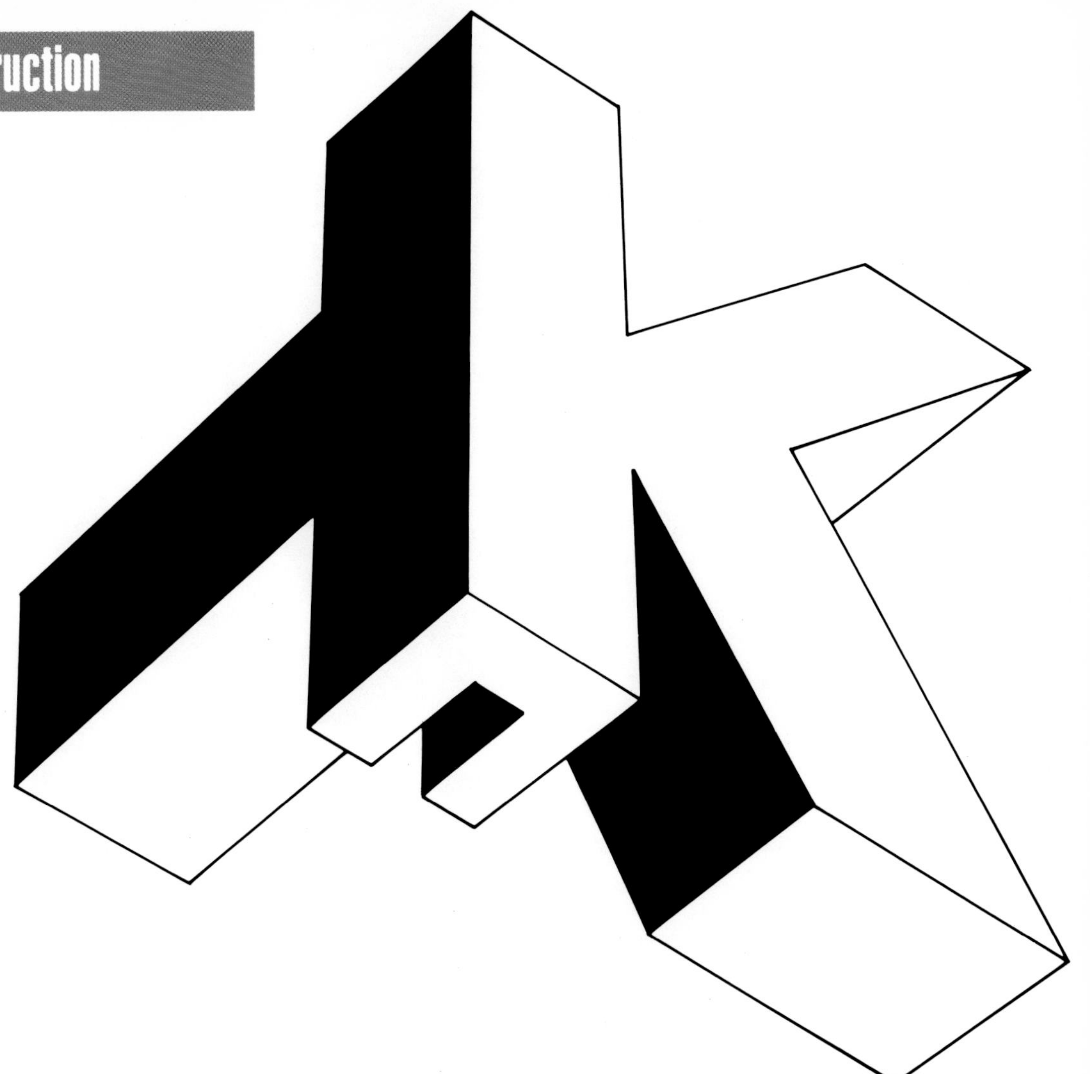

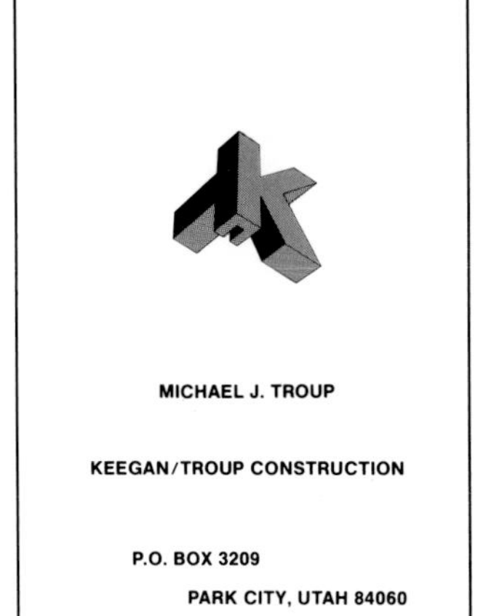

KEEGAN/TROUP CONSTRUCTION

P.O. BOX 3209

PARK CITY

UTAH 84060

WJLA-TV

DESIGNER: Joseph Ford, Baltimore, Maryland

Offit Associates Inc. Investment Counsel
Manhattan Tower 101 East 52 Street New York NY 10022

Offit Associates (Investment Counsellors)

DESIGN FIRM: Kirschner/ Caroff Design, New York, New York

ART DIRECTOR: Lon Kirschner

DESIGNER: Joe Caroff

Heffalump (Imported Children's Toys)

DESIGN FIRM: The Office of Michael Manwaring, San Francisco, California
DESIGNER: Michael Manwaring

Pearson Advertising

1101 Hudson Lane

Suite C

Monroe, Louisiana 71201

Pearson Advertising

1101 Hudson Lane

Suite C

Monroe, Louisiana 71201

318 325 3111

Pearson Advertising

DESIGN FIRM: Loucks Atelier, Inc., Houston, Texas

ART DIRECTOR: Jay Loucks

DESIGNER/ILLUSTRATOR: Morgan Bomar

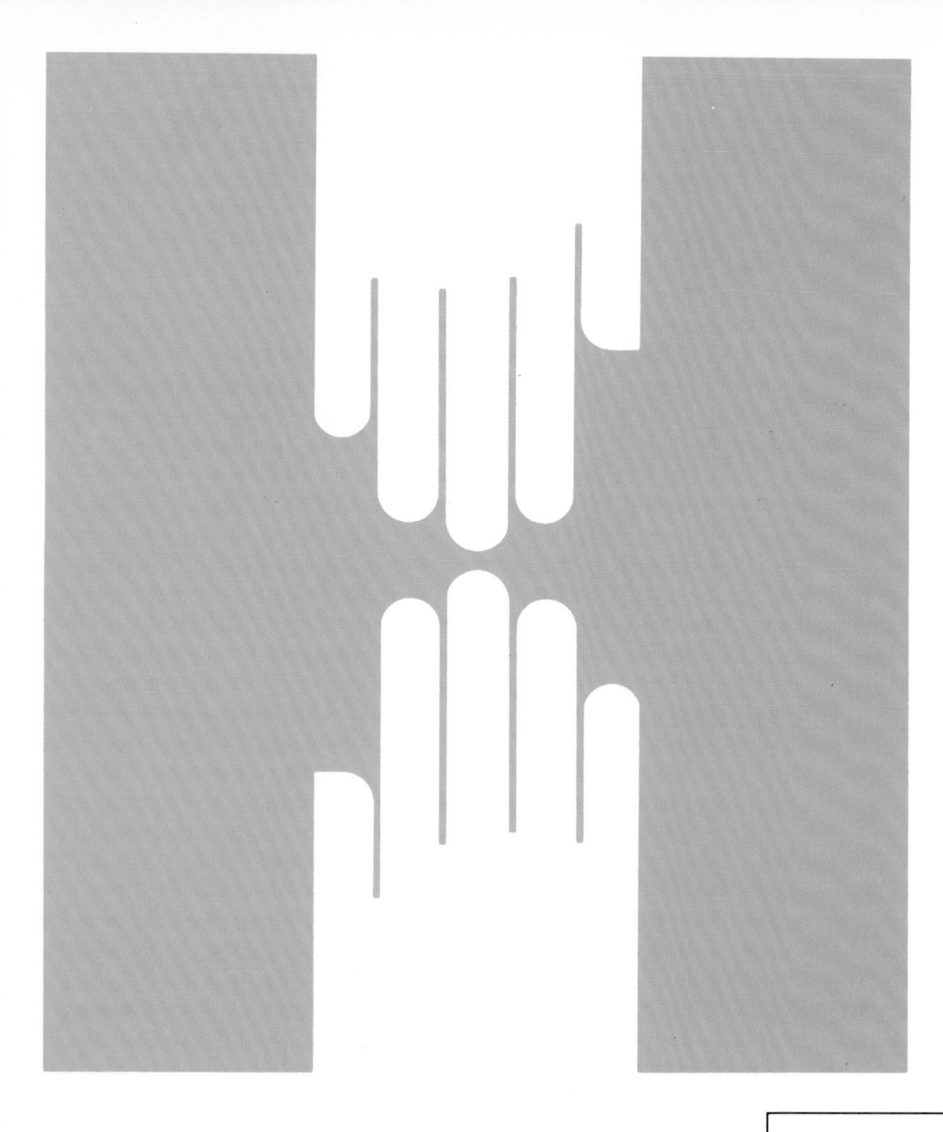

Texas Hospice Organization

DESIGN FIRM: Eisenberg, Inc., Dallas, Texas

ART DIRECTORS: Scott Ray, Arthur Eisenberg

DESIGNER/ILLUSTRATOR: Scott Ray

TEXAS HOSPICE
ORGANIZATION, INC.

P.O. BOX 10998-441
AUSTIN, TEXAS 78766
512 372 9149

Safer Areas for Everyone

A student safety program at Ohio State University.

DESIGN FIRM: The Office of University Publications, Columbus, Ohio

ART DIRECTOR/ DESIGNER: Mark Krumel

SAFER AREAS
FOR EVERYONE

Michael's Restaurant

DESIGN FIRM: D'Auria Design, Bayside, New York

DESIGNER: Karen D'Auria

The Living Leafs Collections

A greeting card and poster production company.

DESIGN FIRM: Rouya Designs, Long Island City, New York

ART DIRECTOR/ DESIGNER/ARTIST: Es Rouya

Norma's Daughters

DESIGNER: Mel Hioki, New York, New York
ILLUSTRATOR: Tom Carnase

Carey Ahrens (Food Broker)

DESIGN FIRM: Hegstrom Design, Campbell, California
DESIGNER/ILLUSTRATOR: Ken Hegstrom

The Art Collector

DESIGN FIRM: CWA Inc./ HumanGraphic, San Diego, California

ART DIRECTOR: Calvin Woo

DESIGNER: Beth Verner

THE COLLECTOR

DESIGN FIRM: Bright & Associates, Santa Monica, California

ART DIRECTORS: Larry Klein, Keith Bright

DESIGNER: Ray Wood

Los Angeles Olympic Organizing Committee Alumni Organization

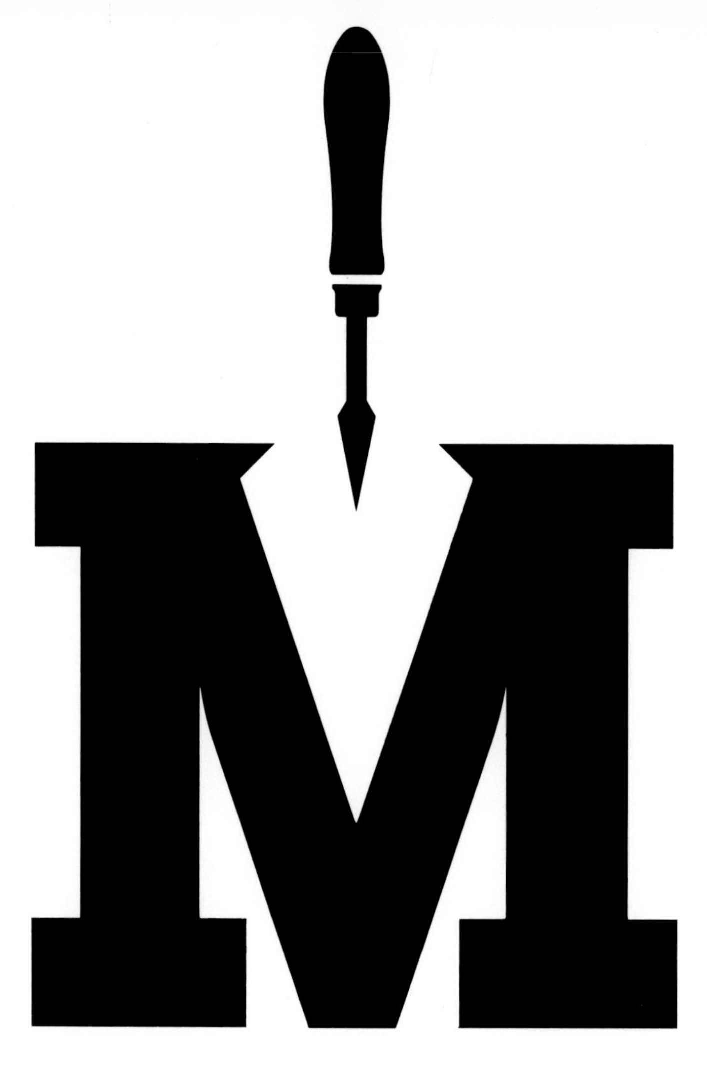

DESIGN FIRM: Smit Ghormley Sanft, Phoenix, Arizona
DESIGNER: Brad Ghormley

The Masonry Co. (Bricklayers)

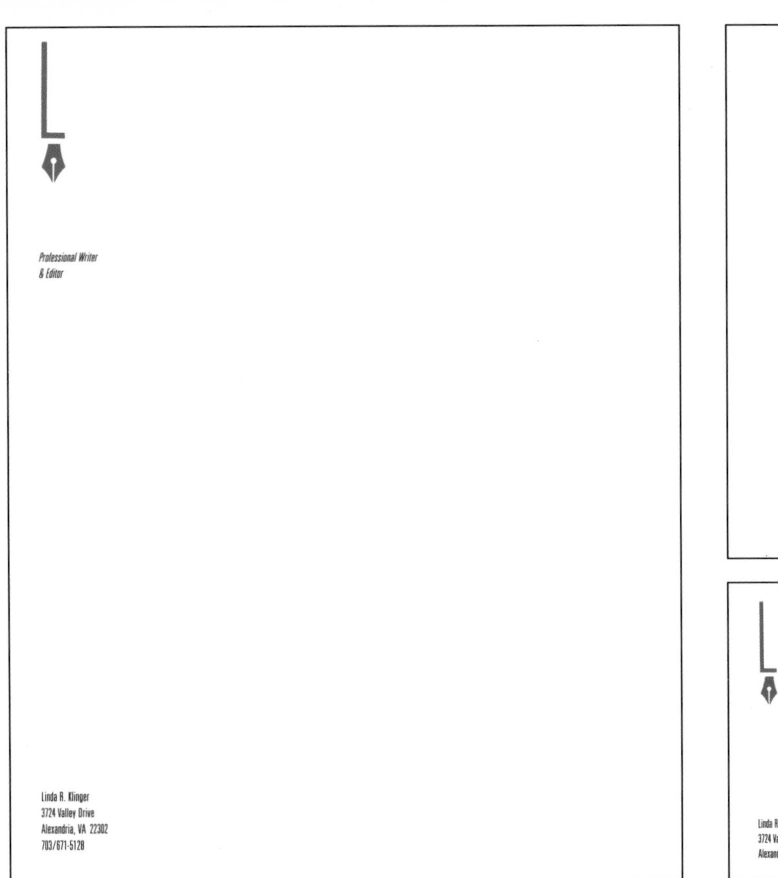

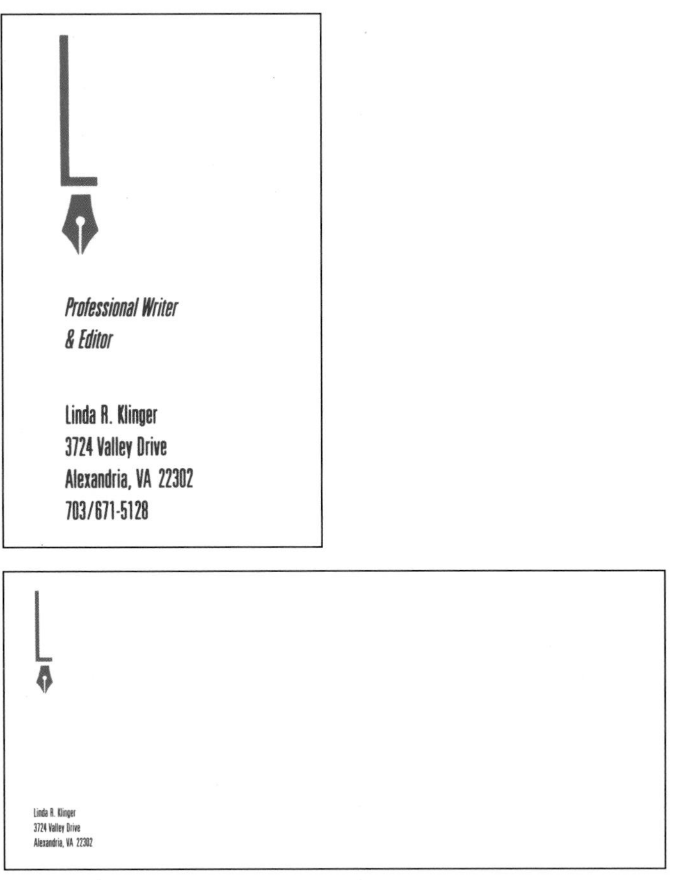

Linda R. Klinger (Professional Writer and Editor)

DESIGN FIRM: Supon Design Group, Washington, D.C.

ART DIRECTOR/ DESIGNER: Supon Phornirunlit

The Aerobic Activity Center (Valentine Racquetball Tournament)

DESIGN FIRM: Richards Brock Miller Mitchel and Associates/The Richards Group, Dallas, Texas
ART DIRECTOR/ DESIGNER: Gary Templin
CALLIGRAPHER: Ken Shafer

Children's Chorus of Oklahoma (Hand-Sign Method Of Teaching Children)

DESIGN FIRM: Walker Creative, Inc., Norman, Oklahoma

DESIGNER/ILLUSTRATOR: Steven Walker

DESIGN FIRM: Rickabaugh Graphics, Columbus, Ohio

DESIGNER: Eric Rickabaugh

DESIGN FIRM: Quinlan Advertising, Indianapolis, Indiana

DESIGNER/ILLUSTRATOR: Pamela Linsley

The Left Bank

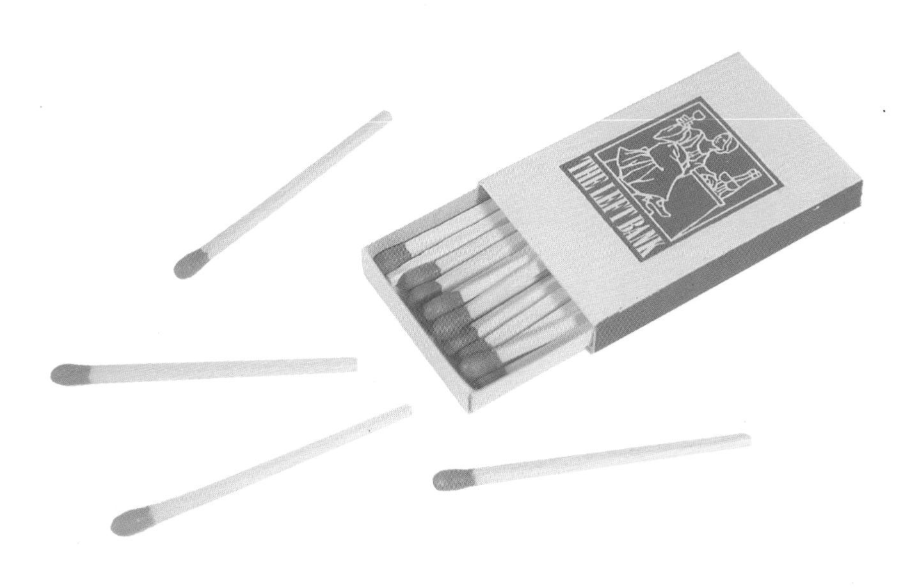

Bent Tree Plaza

DESIGN FIRM: Virginia Morren Design, Dallas, Texas

DESIGNER: Virginia Morren

Mark IV Hair Designs

DESIGN FIRM: MKG Graphic Design, Andalusia, Pennsylvania

DESIGNER: Mary Kay Garttmeier

Suit Yourself

Importers of tailored business wear.

DESIGN FIRM: Don Hammond Design, Ann Arbor, Michigan

ART DIRECTOR: Don Hammond, Jonathon Stewart

DESIGNER: Don Hammond

Fat Chance Records

DESIGN FIRM: Lane Evans Design, Irving, Texas

DESIGNER: Lane Evans

Kathryn E. Buffum, D.D.S.

DESIGN FIRM: Tim Celeski Studios, Seattle, Washington

DESIGNER: Tim Celeski

DESIGN FIRM: Richards Brock Miller Mitchell and Associates/The Richards Group, Dallas, Texas

DESIGNER: D.C. Stipp

Willis Painting Contractor

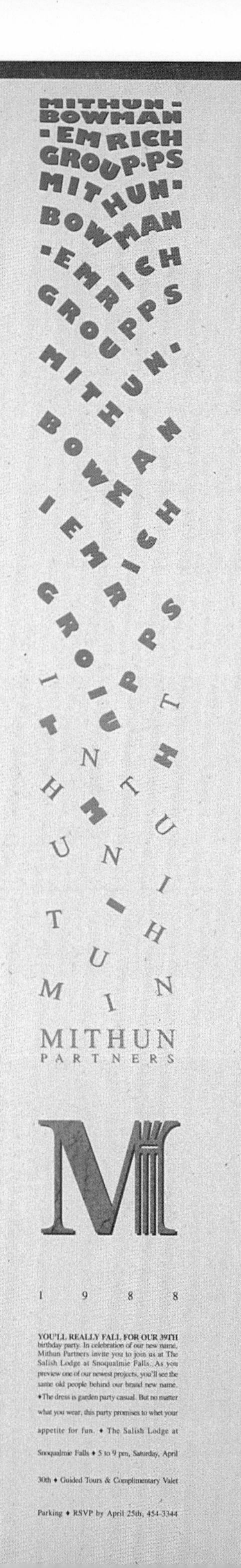

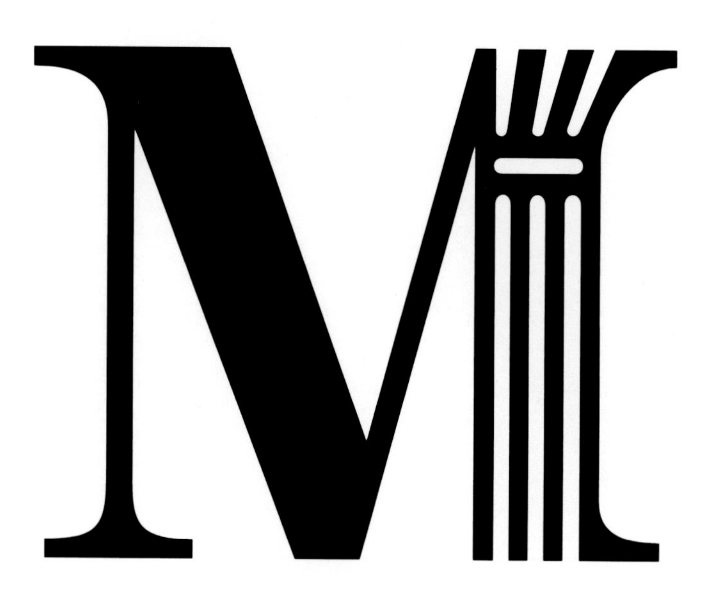

DESIGN FIRM: Hornall Anderson Design Works, Seattle, Washington
ART DIRECTOR: Jack Anderson
DESIGNERS: Jack Anderson, Cliff Chung, Brian O'Neill

Mithun Partners (Architects)

Los Angeles Chapter of American Institute of Architects

DESIGNER: Dan Nicklasson, Los Angeles, California

LA/AIA

OFFICERS

Donald C. Axon, AIA
President

Cyril Chern, AIA
Vice President

Richard A. Appel, AIA
Secretary

Robert S. Harris, FAIA
Treasurer

DIRECTORS

Mark W. Hall, AIA

Fernando Juarez, AIA

John Mutlow, AIA

Barton Phelps, AIA

Robert Reed, AIA

Norma M. Sklarek, FAIA

Chester A. Widom, AIA

Lawrence A. Robbins, AIA
President, SFV Section

R. D. McDonnell
Associate Director

Heidi Moore
President, WAL

Janice Axon
Executive Director

Los Angeles Chapter/American Institute of Architects, 8687 Melrose Avenue, Los Angeles, California 90069 213/659 2282

The Black Sheep

The Black Sheep (Hand-Knit Woolens Store)

DESIGN FIRM: David Lausch Graphics, Baltimore, Maryland

DESIGNERS: David Lausch, Debbie Shaull

Black Sheep Woolens

DESIGN FIRM:

KaiserDicken, Burlington, Vermont

DESIGNER: Debra Kaiser

PRINTING: Atelier Graphics

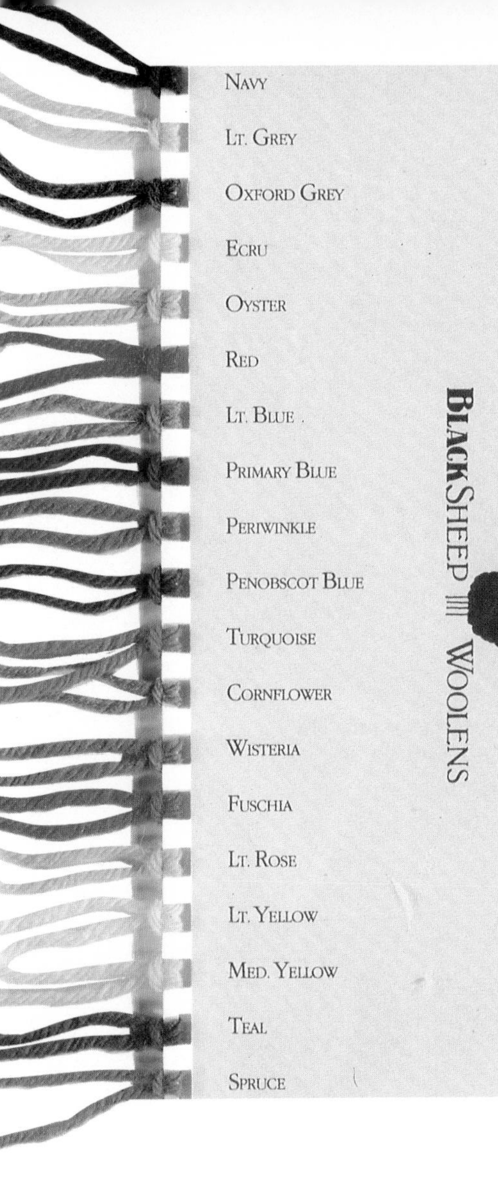

Headbands & Hats

1989

Warmth
Quality
Unique Designs
Wonderful Colors
Made in Vermont

BLACKSHEEP WOOLENS

What's New at the...

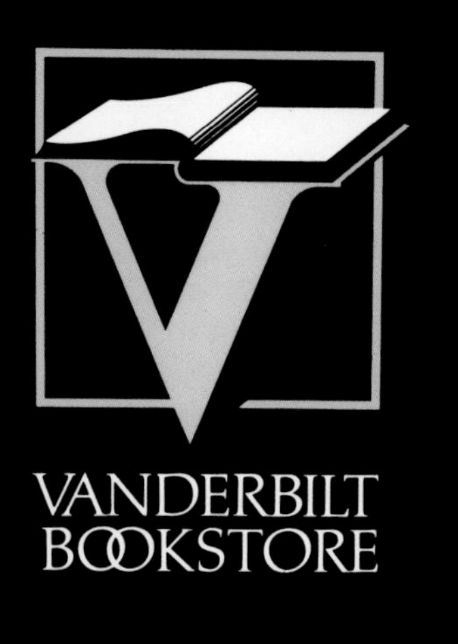

Vanderbilt University Bookstore

DESIGN FIRM: I.D. Image Design, Nashville, Tennessee

DESIGNER: Howard Diehl

Welcome to the newly-renovated Vanderbilt Bookstore. We invite you to come in, look around, and see what's new!

You'll discover a completely fresh approach to serving you. The Vanderbilt Bookstore is designed to afford the convenience, variety and quality of a large department store, enhanced with the priority of providing superior customer service. We offer an exhaustive stock of merchandise for the discriminating buyer. This merchandise is organized into departments to assist you in locating what you need quickly. You will find everything you need to ensure the most enjoyable campus shopping available.

2730 Scott Boulevard
Santa Clara, CA 95050
(408) 496-0755

Lightning
Printing

2730 Scott Boulevard
Santa Clara, CA 95050
(408) 496-0755

Lightning Printing

DESIGN FIRM: Hegstrom Design, Campbell, California

DESIGNER/ILLUSTRATOR: Ken Hegstrom

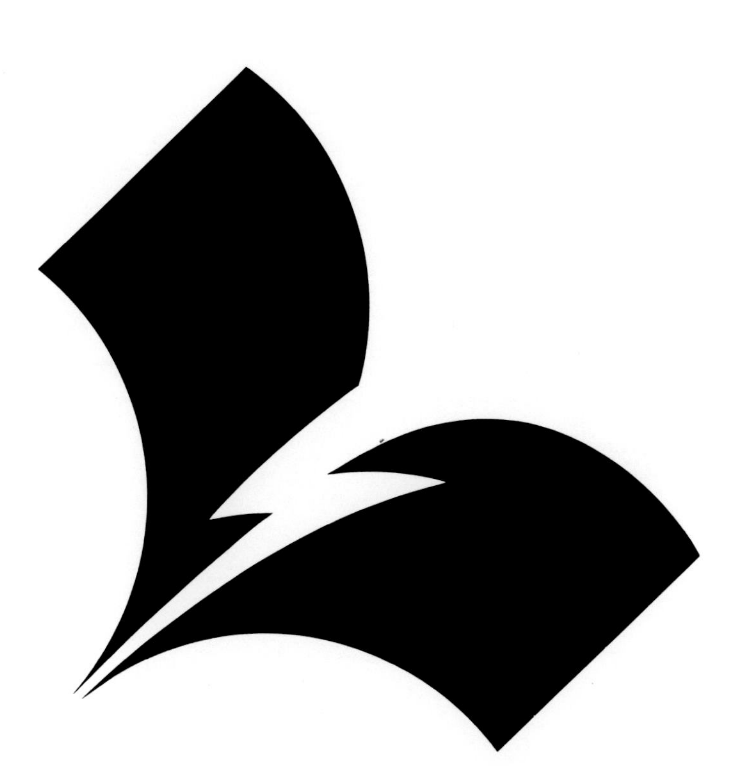

2730 Scott Boulevard
Santa Clara, CA 95050
(408) 496-0755

Design for Health

DESIGN FIRM: Flanagan-Thomas Design, Santa Clara, California

DESIGNER: Craig Thomas

Fitzroy's Lounge

DESIGN FIRM: Robinson Advertising & Marketing, Memphis, Tennessee

ART DIRECTOR/ DESIGNER: David Meyer

HANDLETTERING: Beth Mitchell

Blind Dog Graphics

DESIGN FIRM:

Montgomery and Partners, Inc., Reading, Pennsylvania

DESIGNER: Steven Fabian

BLIND DOG GRAPHICS™

Reubens Meats

DESIGN FIRM: Mitchell Lindgren, Minneapolis, Minnesota

ART DIRECTOR: Bob Frink

DESIGNER/ILLUSTRATOR: Mitchell Lindgren

DESIGN FIRM: Lynne Cannoy Design/Illustration, Pittsburgh, Pennsylvania

ART DIRECTOR/ DESIGNER/ILLUSTRATOR: Lynne Cannoy

COPYWRITERS: Vince DeCarlucci, Karen DeCarlucci

EVA GABOR'S SOLUTION TO THE "WHAT AM I GONNA DO WITH MY HAIR?" BLUES Nº 2

The Blues: "My hair is a wreck... it's dull and damaged, but I'm afraid to cut it. I wonder how shorter hair would look."
The Solution: Short wigs are versatile, refreshing and more wearable than they have ever been. We show you two or three suggested looks, but every Eva Gabor wig can be combed into many different variations by adding your own personal styling touches. Softly frame your face with "MiLady" for a flattering, younger look; order "Spotlight" if you enjoy a natural looking, classic style like Eva wears. This is a great way to experiment... it's easy and these reduced prices make it very economical.

How exciting... a brand new year has started and we all have the opportunity to make it the best ever! But, isn't it interesting how at this time of year we all feel restless—ready for a change?

So many years of being involved with the hair fashion business has taught us that just a change in your hair style is the easiest and most effective way to give yourself that extra boost you need to look and feel your very best!

Last year, I received so many encouraging letters from THE WIG COMPANY customers, sharing with me how their Eva Gabor wigs have, in some way, been an asset. Their reasons are as simple as saving a little time to do something more pleasurable than fussing with their hair; or many enjoy having a chance to wear flattering new styles that they cannot achieve with their own hair, and some reasons were as special as helping them through the trauma of medical hair loss.

Knowing your needs is important to me and the dedicated people at THE WIG COMPANY. Our goal for 1985 is to implement the most wanted personal services based on what we hear and read from our customers. We know that if we listen to what you want... then you'll be more delighted than ever with our products and our service... that's when I'll be satisfied that we're doing a super job.

To start toward our goal, we have taken a serious look at your hair and wig problems. My staff nicknamed them the "what am I gonna do with my hair blues?"... but we didn't stop there, we have free and easy solutions for all your hair problems in this issue!

So, make a cup of tea, curl up on the sofa, and enjoy!

Cordially,
Karen
Karen DeCarlucci

MILADY

From the look that captured the heart of Prince Charles, Eva Gabor created Milady. It has the casual freshness of youth, plus the easy comfort needed by today's contemporary woman. Sleek, full front accents beautiful eyes. Soft sides that sweep back to a long neckline flatter the profile. Adjustable—average to smaller head size. H324

Regular Price $5[illegible].00
Sale Price $33.99

COLORS: 18, 2, 4, 6, 8, 10, 12, 14, 16, 18, 20, 22, E23, 24, 27, 30, 33, 38, 44, 51, 56, 60, 17/101, 18/22, 24/14

SPOTLIGHT

Brings Hollywood glamour and feminine beauty back to hair design. You don't have to be a star to be in the spotlight—just wear Eva Gabor's own style: Spotlight! It's soft, natural, and easy to manage with a hand-tied front and baby hairs giving an ultra-natural hairline. Adjustable—average to smaller head size. H361

Regular Price $4[illegible].00
Sale Price $32.99

COLORS: 18, 2, 4, 6, 8, 10, 12, 14, 16, 18, 22, E23, 24, 27, 30, 33, 38, 44, 51, 56, 60, 17/101, 18/22, 24/14

CREDIT CARD USERS CALL TOLL FREE 1 800 245-6288
Instant Credit Card Ordering Visa/MasterCard
In Pennsylvania Call Collect (412) 344-3882
8:30 a.m. to 7:00 p.m. weekdays
10:00 a.m. to 5:00 p.m. Saturday

2

EVA GABOR'S SOLUTION TO THE "WHAT AM I GONNA DO WITH MY HAIR?" BLUES Nº 3

The Blues: "I'm so proud of my long hair and don't want to cut it, but it's not always practical, and there are so many new short styles that I like."
The Solution: Short wigs are so pretty and practical. Eva Gabor has many to choose from... here are just a few that look great on most women! Best of all—practical doesn't have to be boring—these flattering short styles are as versatile as you wish. With a flick of a brush you can get just the look you want. Here are a few ways to wear our three favorites. "Nugget" is chic and dressy. "Gambit" is a sculptured boy cut. "Whisper" has the latest swept-back styling.

NUGGET

BEST BUY!

Eva Gabor knows it is right in step with this season's dressy mood. The petal curl top and swept back sides end at a full nape. Lovely, sculptured NUGGET makes wig wearing what it is meant to be... as fun and chic as it is super fitting and easy-care. Adjustable—average to smaller head size. H328

Regular Price $5[illegible].00
Sale Price $24.99

COLORS: 18, 2, 4, 6, 8, 10, 12, 14, 16, 18, 22, E23, 24, 27, 30, 33, 38, 44, 51, 56, 60, 101, 17/101, 18/22, 24/14, 307, 280, 118

GAMBIT

Eva Gabor's no-bulge sculptured look. The style is a short boy cut with Perma-lift™ on top for extra body. Sides come forward or sweep back. PermaTease® sides for fullness. Adjustable—average to smaller head size. H316

Regular Price $4[illegible].00
Sale Price $36.99

COLORS: 18, 2, 4, 6, 8, 10, 12, 14, 16, 18, 22, E23, 24, 26, 27, 30, 33, 38, 44, 51, 56, 60, 101, 130, 17/101, 18/22, 24/14

WHISPER

BEST BUY!

This swept back hair fashion with a tapered neckline will keep you up to date with hair styling trends. New "thin weft" construction results in a light, natural wig without a stiff "wiggy" appearance. "Whisper" is just a matter of brush and go! Adjustable—average to larger head size. H366

Regular Price $5[illegible].00
Sale Price $19.99

COLORS: 18, 2, 4, 6, 8, 10, 12, 14, 16, 18, 22, E23, 24, 27, 30, 33, 38, 44, 51, 56, 60, 101, 17/101, 18/22, 24/14, 280, 502

100% GUARANTEE
If an Eva Gabor wig and our service isn't everything you expected, return your wig within thirty days for a prompt refund or exchange... whichever you prefer.

the Wig company.

3

The Wig Company

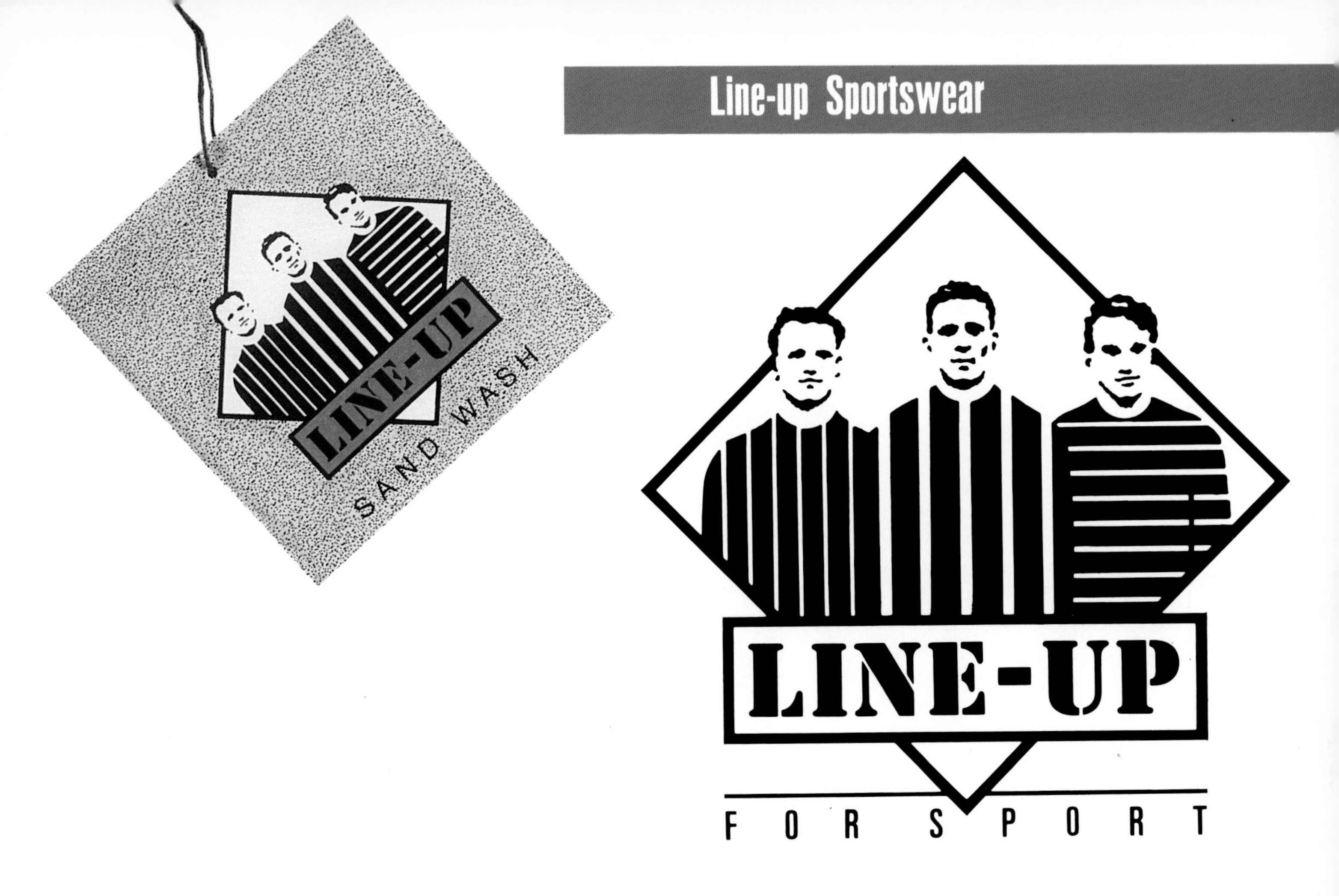

DESIGNER: Marjorie Dotson, La Jolla, California

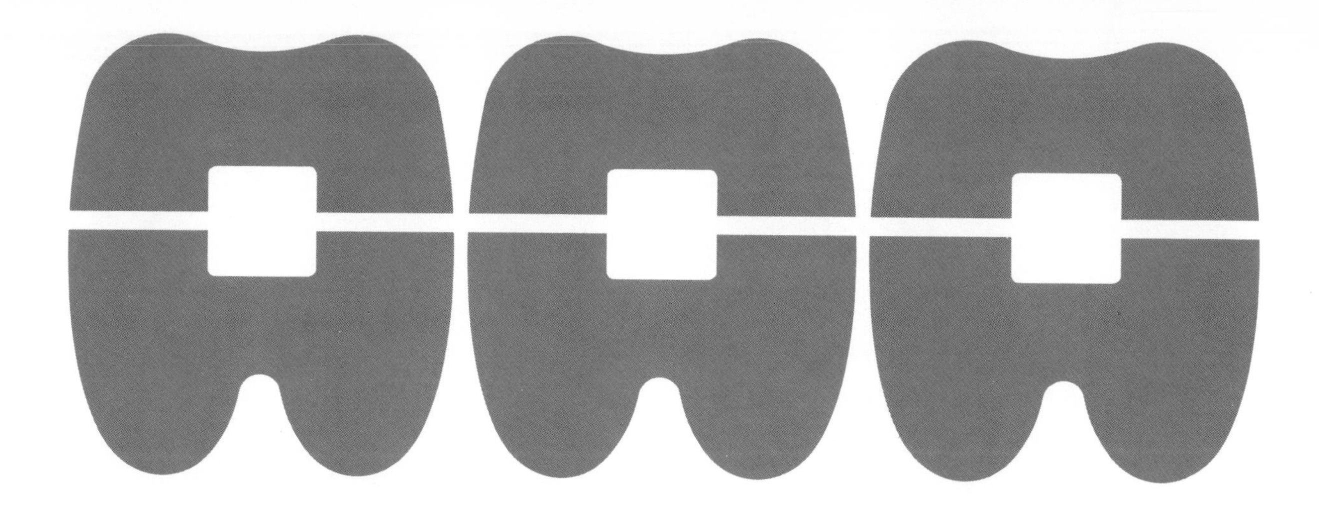

Morton Weyler & Mark Schpero, Orthodontics

DESIGN FIRM: Carangelo Design, Middletown, Connecticut

DESIGNER: Rob Carangelo

A real-estate management, design and construction firm.

DESIGN FIRM: Beckenstein Enterprise New York, New York

DESIGNER: Arthur Beckenstein

Beckenstein Enterprises

Beckenstein Enterprises

Beckenstein Enterprises
PO Box 8228
183 Prestige Park Road
East Hartford, CT 06108
203/289-7924

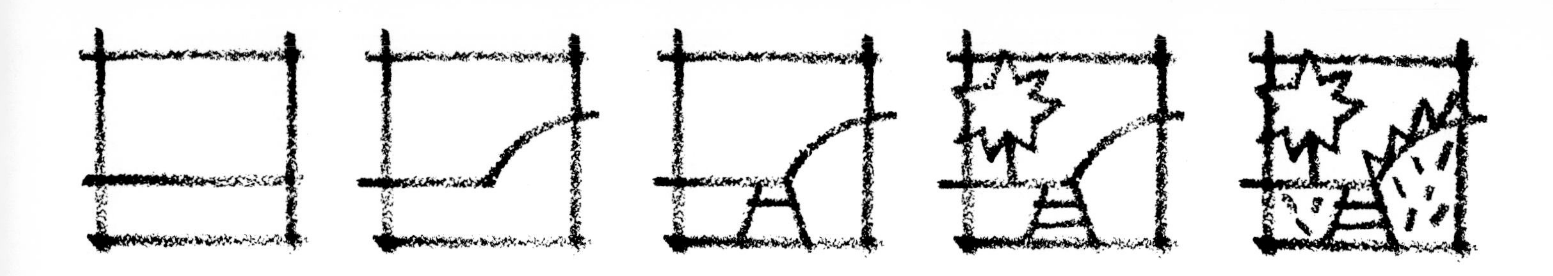

Brink Biechlin (Landscape Architect)

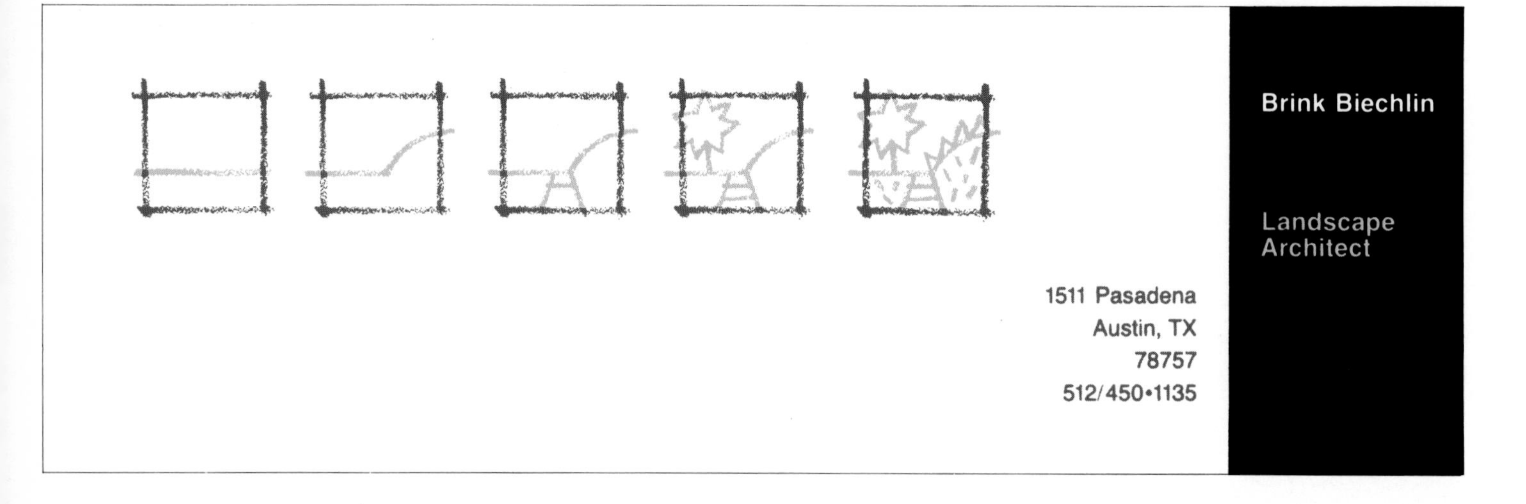

Brink Biechlin
Landscape Architect
1511 Pasadena
Austin, TX
78757
512 450•1135

Brink Biechlin
1511 Pasadena
Austin, TX
78757

DESIGN FIRM: Roger Christian & Co., San Antonio, Texas
ART DIRECTOR/ DESIGNER: Mark Wilcox
ILLUSTRATORS: Mark Wilcox, David Hackney

DESIGN FIRM: Champlin Alexander, Portland, Oregon

DESIGNERS: Doug Alexander, Dale Champlin

ILLUSTRATOR: Dale Champlin

Oregon's quality fishing experience with Jeff & Ken Helfrich

Ken and Jeff Helfrich (Fishing Guides)

Weight Management Systems

Gary A. Moore, M.D., F.A.A.F.P.
Medical Director, Bariatric Medicine

Water Tower Place, Suite 822
845 North Michigan Avenue
Chicago, Illinois 60611
Telephone: (312) 943-6100

DESIGNER/ILLUSTRATOR:

Rosanne Lobes, Chicago, Illinois

Weight Management Systems

Sports
Psychology

ROTELLA
ASSOCIATES

P.O. Box 845
Rutland, Vermont 05701

Sports
Psychology

ROTELLA
ASSOCIATES

P.O. Box 845
Rutland, Vermont 05701

Rotella Associates (Sports Psychologist)

DESIGN FIRM: Design Design Ltd., Rutland, Vermont
ART DIRECTOR: Maria Riley
DESIGNERS: Art Bemis, Debby Bradder

Ice Company of Elmira

A wholesaler of block and cubed ice.

DESIGN FIRM: MarcAnthony Design Group, Syracuse, New York

DESIGNER: Marc Slawson

Right Connection (Business Phone Systems)

DESIGNER: Michael Del Gigante, Brooklyn, New York

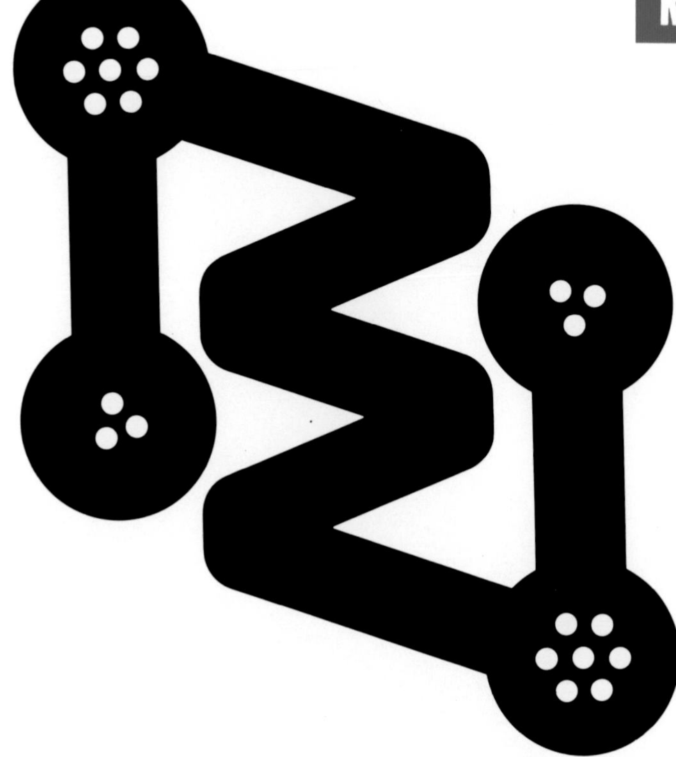

First Presbyterian Church Day Care Nursey

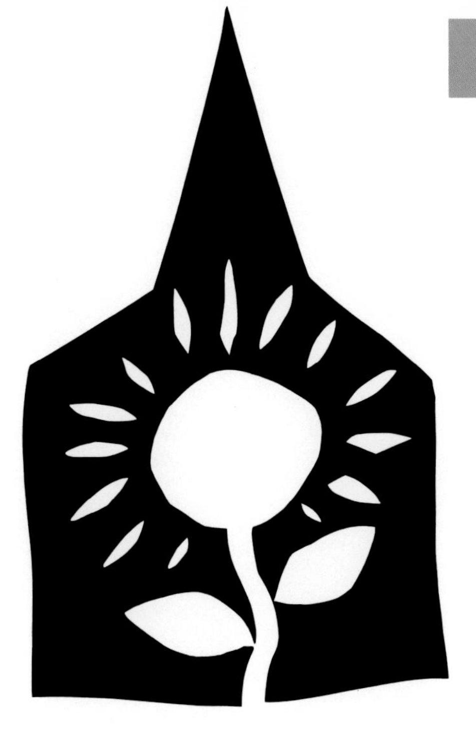

DESIGN FIRM: Mark Oliver, Inc., Santa Barbara, California

ART DIRECTOR: Mark Oliver

DESIGNERS: Mark Oliver and Susan Edelmann-Adams

Theatre Tulsa Team Tennis Tournament

DESIGN FIRM: Advertising, Inc., Tulsa, Oklahoma

DESIGNER/ILLUSTRATOR: Mick Thurber

Decatur Memorial Foundation

DESIGN FIRM: CS&A,

Normal, Illinois

ART DIRECTOR/

DESIGNER: Wendy

Behrens

CREATIVE DIRECTOR/

COPYWRITER: Kim Urban

ACCOUNT EXECUTIVE:

Gail Dobbins

SCULPTOR: Larry

Wetherholt

ONE LIFE ENRICHES MANY

ART DIRECTOR/ DESIGNER/ILLUSTRATOR: Vicki Gullickson, Denver, Colorado

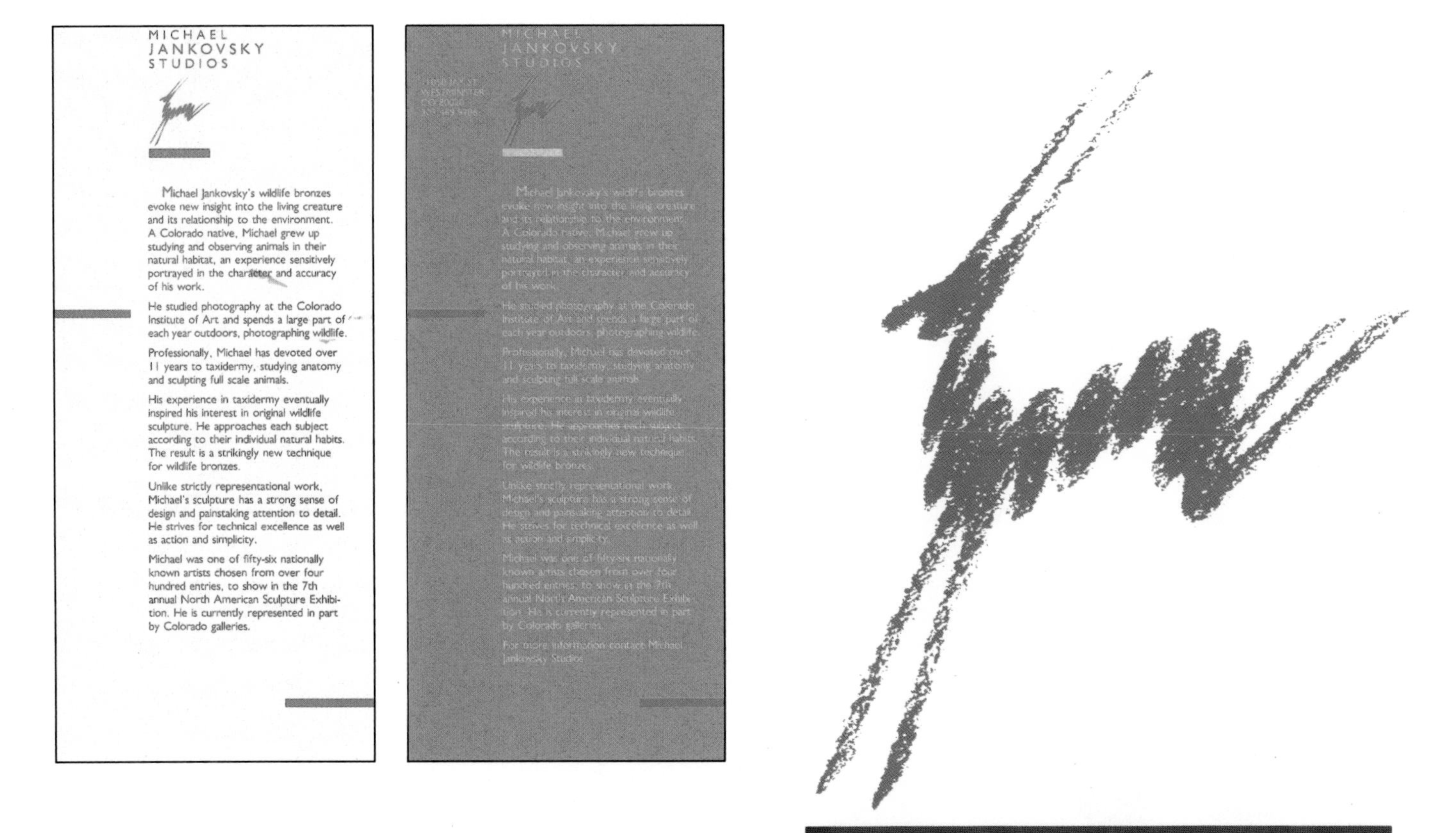

MICHAEL
JANKOVSKY
STUDIOS

Michael Jankovsky's wildlife bronzes evoke new insight into the living creature and its relationship to the environment. A Colorado native, Michael grew up studying and observing animals in their natural habitat, an experience sensitively portrayed in the character and accuracy of his work.

He studied photography at the Colorado Institute of Art and spends a large part of each year outdoors, photographing wildlife.

Professionally, Michael has devoted over 11 years to taxidermy, studying anatomy and sculpting full scale animals.

His experience in taxidermy eventually inspired his interest in original wildlife sculpture. He approaches each subject according to their individual natural habits. The result is a strikingly new technique for wildlife bronzes.

Unlike strictly representational work, Michael's sculpture has a strong sense of design and painstaking attention to detail. He strives for technical excellence as well as action and simplicity.

Michael was one of fifty-six nationally known artists chosen from over four hundred entries, to show in the 7th annual North American Sculpture Exhibition. He is currently represented in part by Colorado galleries.

DESIGN FIRM: The Harvard Group, New York, New York

DESIGNER: Peter Wong

ILLUSTRATOR: Jim Caulfield

Home
Government Securities Fund
Fact Sheet

1. **Investment goal**
   - High current income with low risk to principal

2. **Key sales features**
   - Designed for the investor/saver who wants income with low risk to principal
   - Offers potential for high current monthly income; monthly dividend checks
   - Invests primarily in securities backed by full faith and credit of US Government, its agencies and instrumentalities (Note: Shares of the Fund are not backed by any government guarantees and the value of Fund shares will fluctuate.)

3. **Special Account Executive incentive program**
   - 60% Account Executive payout through 8/24/88 based on the following commission schedule

Investment	Sales Charge	Normal Dealer Reallowance	Special Dealer Reallowance Through 8/24/88
Less than $100,000	4.75%	4.25%	4.75%
$100,000 but less than $250,000	4.00	3.50	4.00
$250,000 but less than $500,000	3.00	2.50	3.00
$500,000 but less than $1,000,000	2.00	1.60	2.00
$1,000,000 but less than $2,000,000	1.00	0.80	1.00
$2,000,000 but less than $4,000,000	0.50	0.40	0.50
$4,000,000 and over	0.00*	0.00	0.00

- 25 basis point trail program paid on assets that remain invested for a period of one year
- Award and trip incentive program through 8/24/88

* Brokers may be paid a commission of at least 0.15% of the offering price on investments of $4,000,000 or more.

For Internal Use Only

An
Exciting
Investment
Opportunity...

DESIGN FIRM: Medical Media Graphics, St. Paul, Minnesota

DESIGNER: Timothy Trost

School for Ophthalmic Technicians
St. Paul-Ramsey Medical Center
St. Paul, Minnesota

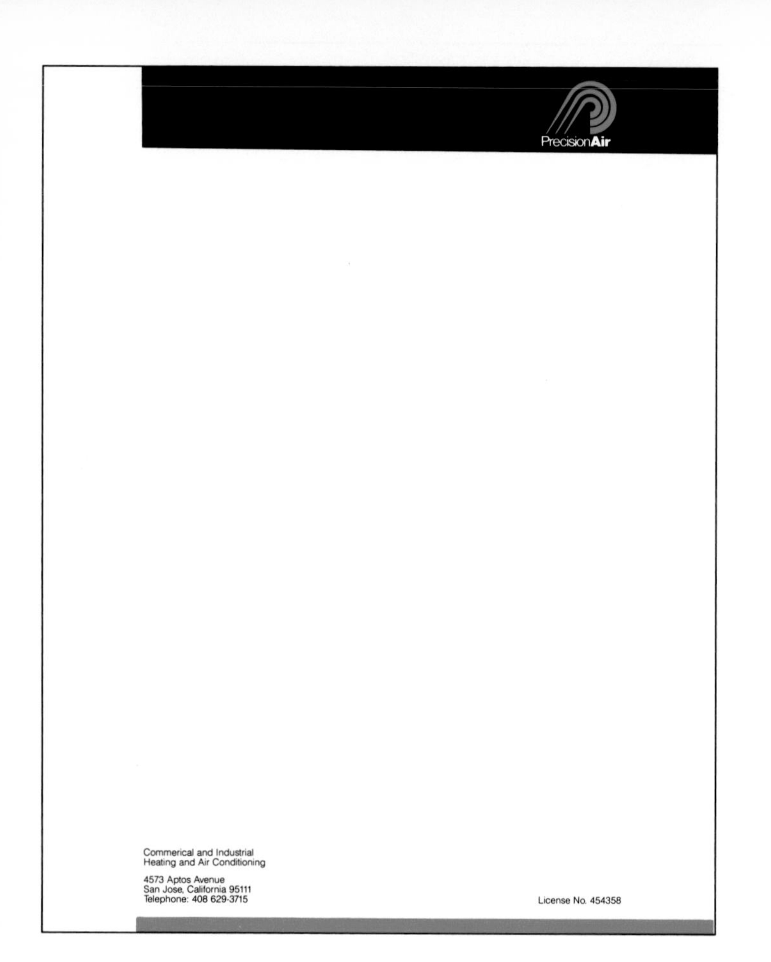

Precision Air (Heating And Air Conditioning Contractor)

DESIGN FIRM: Hegstrom Design, Campbell, California

DESIGNER/ILLUSTRATOR: Ken Hegstrom

DESIGN FIRM: Jann Church Partners, Newport Beach, California

ART DIRECTORS/ DESIGNERS: Jann Church, Shelly Beck

Century Centre

Great American Food Restaurant

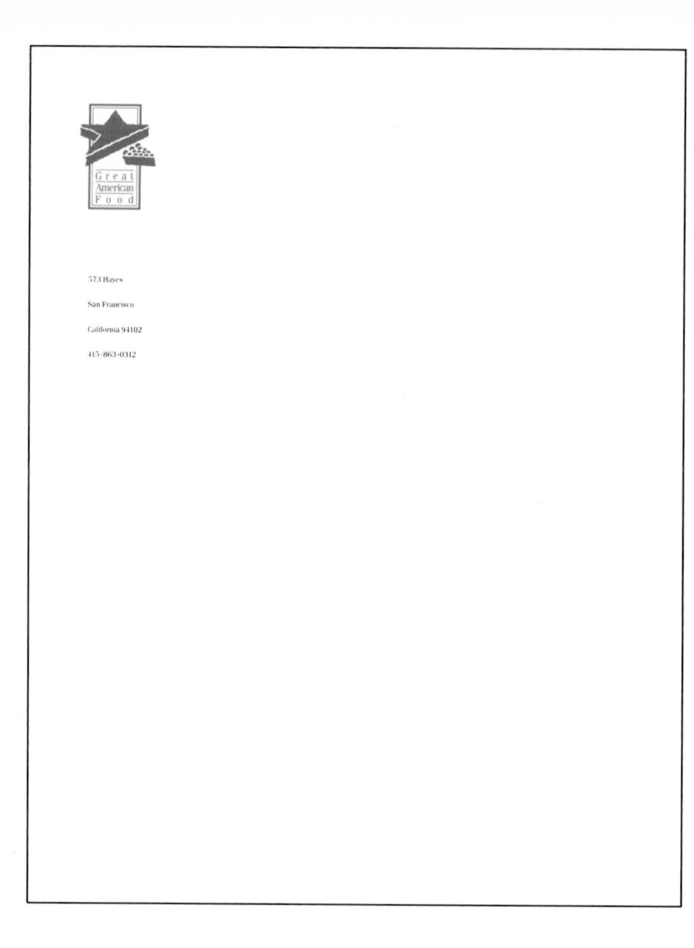

DESIGNER: Bruce A. Yelaska, San Francisco, California

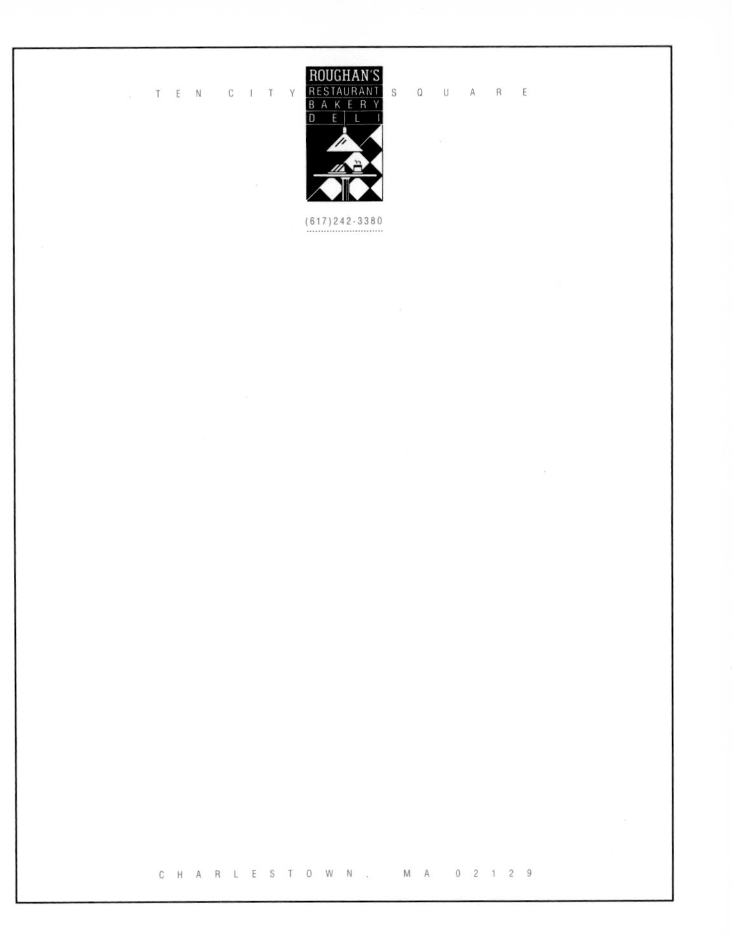

Roughan's Restaurant

DESIGN FIRM: Runnion Design, Lynnfield, Massachusetts

ART DIRECTOR/DESIGNER/ILLUSTRATOR: Jeff Runnion

M E N U

ROUGHAN'S
RESTAURANT
BAKERY
DELI

MONDAY

TUESDAY

WEDNESDAY

THURSDAY

FRIDAY

Crosswind Horns

DESIGNER: Catherine Carrier, Charlotte, North Carolina

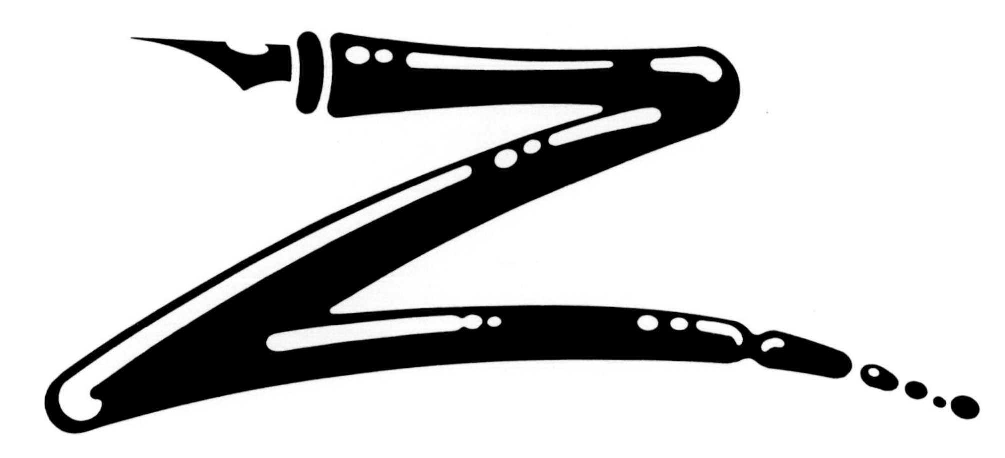

DESIGN FIRM: Graphics Network, Long Beach, California

DESIGNER: Michael Scanlan

ILLUSTRATOR: Tom Cutter

Zemkie Copywriting

Blossoms of Silk

Custom silk flower arrangement.

DESIGN FIRM: DeOlivera Creative, Inc., Denver, Colorado

ART DIRECTOR: Richard A. DeOlivera

DESIGNER: Richard J. Tackett

Peeples Brothers Construction

DESIGN FIRM: Don Faia Design, Los Gatos, California

ART DIRECTOR/ DESIGNER/ILLUSTRATOR: Don Faia

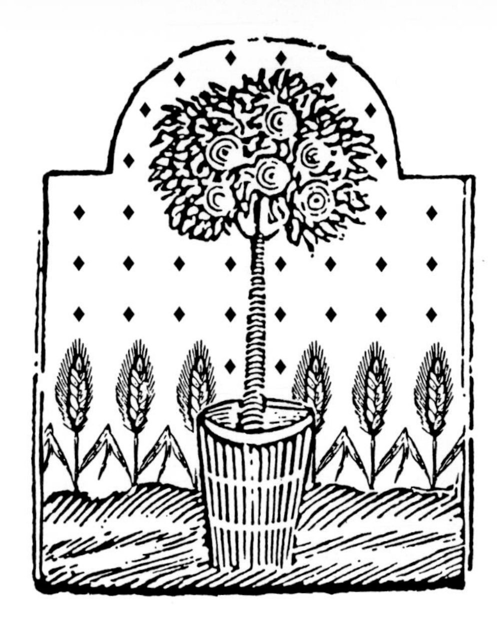

COUNTRY LIFE

VEGETARIAN BUFFET

Country Life

DESIGN FIRM: White & Associates, Los Angeles, California

DESIGNER/ILLUSTRATOR: Ken White

DESIGN FIRM: Corey & Co., Watertown, Massachusetts
ART DIRECTOR/ ILLUSTRATOR: Scott Nash
DESIGNER: Scott Nash, Kyoko Tanika

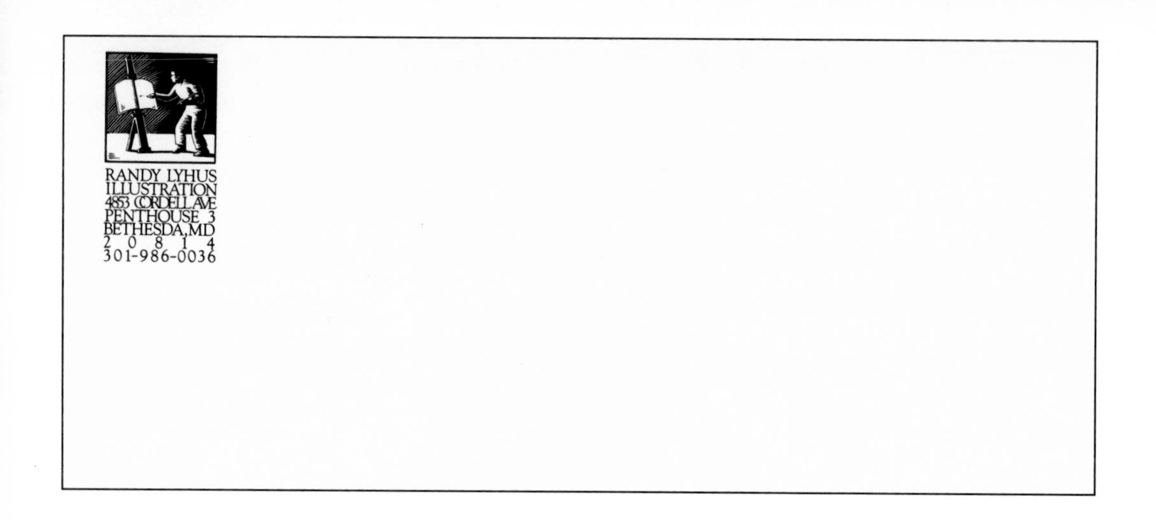

Randy Lyhus (Illustrator)

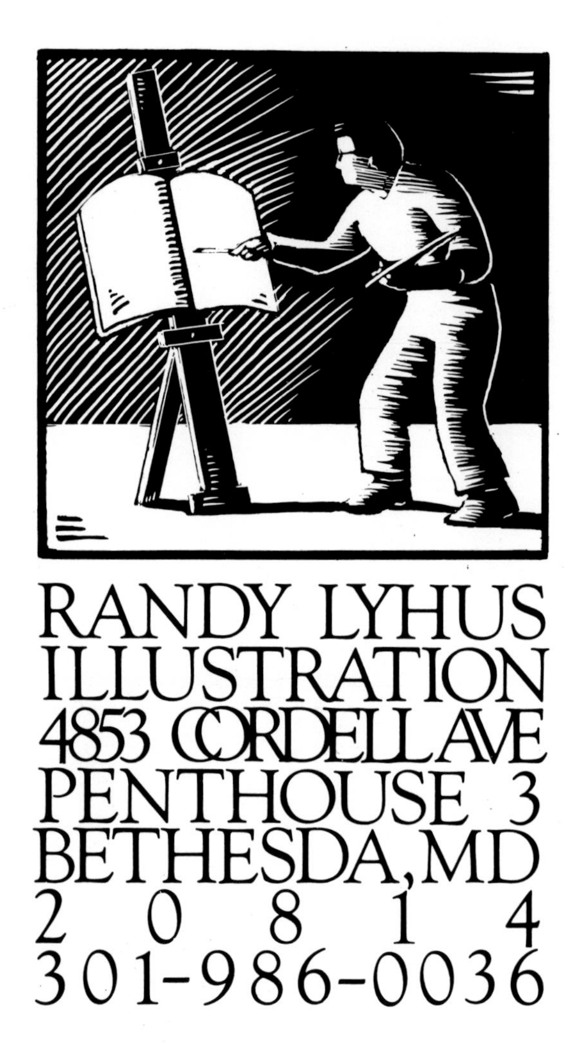

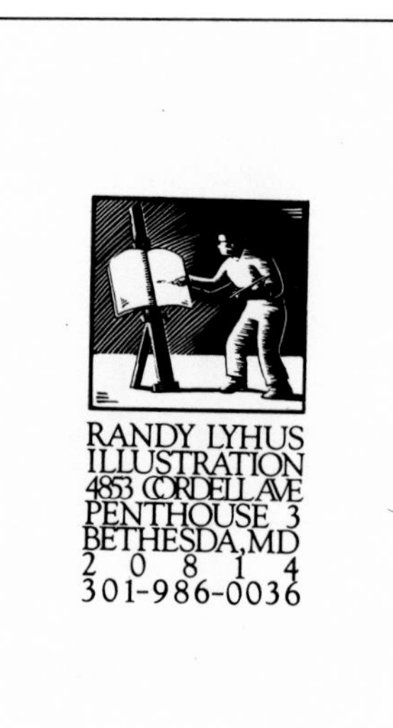

DESIGN FIRM: Randy Lyhus Illustration, Bethesda, Maryland

DESIGNER: Randy Lyhus

Morren + Barkin (Publishers)

DESIGN FIRM: Virginia Morren Design, Dallas, Texas

ART DIRECTOR: Virginia Morren

DESIGNER: Brian Morren

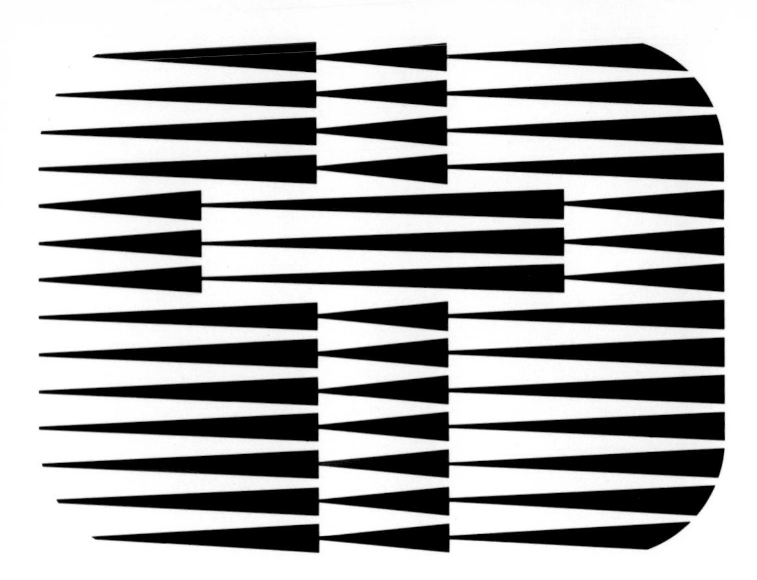

Lakewood Church TV Productions

DESIGN FIRM: Steven Sessions, Inc., Houston, Texas

ART DIRECTOR/ DESIGNER: Steven Sessions

ILLUSTRATOR: Jesus Felix

Lakewood Television Productions
P.O. Box 23000
Houston, Texas 77228
713/635-3226

Shipping Address:
7417 East Houston Road
Houston, Texas 77028

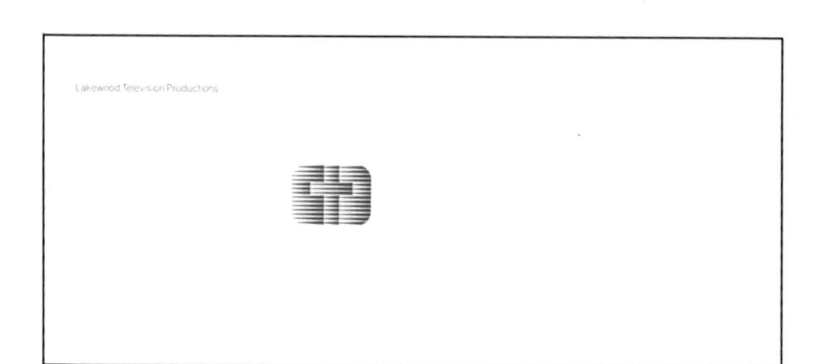

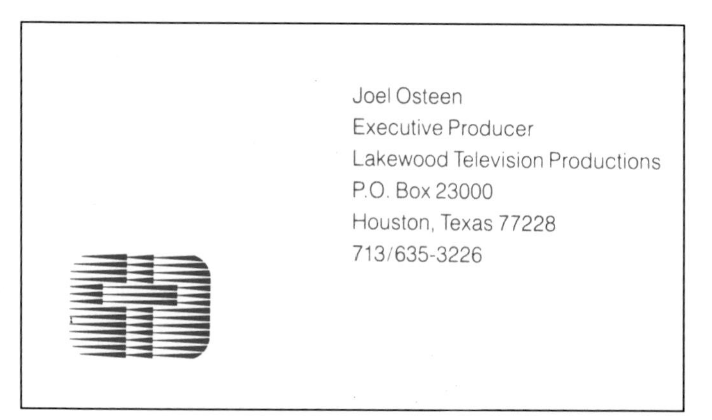

First Bank Systems (Annual Managers Conference)

DESIGN FIRM: Duffy Design Group, Minneapolis, Minnesota
ART DIRECTOR/ DESIGNER/ILLUSTRATOR: Charles S. Anderson

DESIGN FIRM: Dann Snapp Design, Chicago, Illinois

ART DIRECTOR/ DESIGNER: Dann Snapp

Harbert . . . Creative

Dr. Daniel E. Rush
Chiropractic Physician
725 East Broadway Road
Mesa, Arizona 85204
(602) 964-4652

DESIGN FIRM: Art Lofgreen Design, Tempe, Arizona

DESIGNER: Art Lofgreen

Dr. Daniel F. Rush, Chiropractor

Dr. Daniel E. Rush
Chiropractic Physician
725 East Broadway Road
Mesa, Arizona 85204

Voice Shuttle

A business radio satellite communications firm.

DESIGN FIRM: Grayson Design Group, Hightstown, New Jersey

ART DIRECTOR/ DESIGNER: Fletcher Grayson

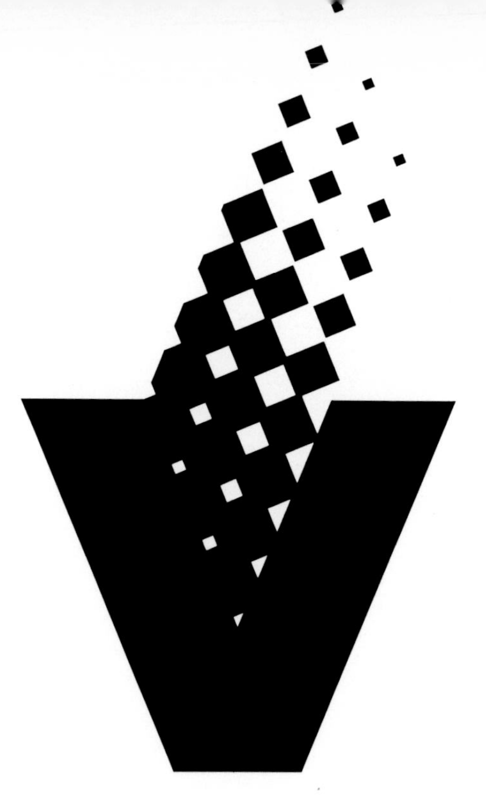

Desert Mountain Development

DESIGN FIRM: Hubbard and Hubbard Design, Phoenix, Arizona

DESIGNER: Ann Morton

Gulf Health Corporation

DESIGNER: Lynne Wells,

Decatur, Alabama

Alpha Omega (Booklet Printer)

DESIGN FIRM: Hegstrom

Design, Campbell,

California

DESIGNER/ILLUSTRATOR:

Ken Hegstrom

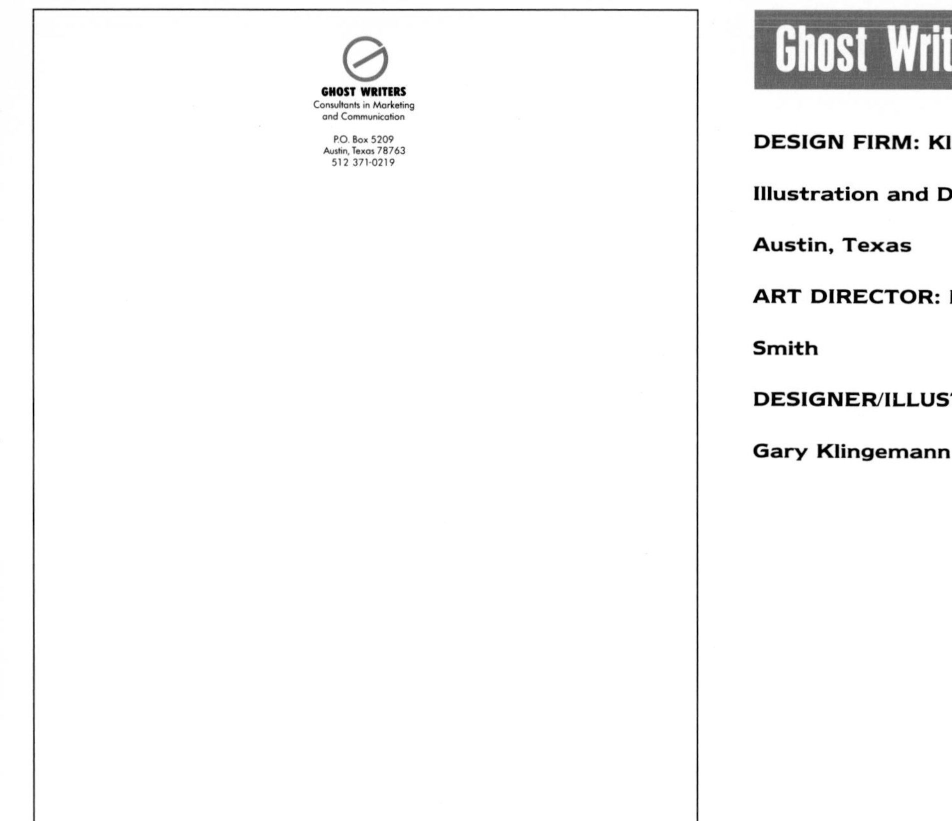

Ghost Writers

DESIGN FIRM: Klingemann Illustration and Design, Austin, Texas
ART DIRECTOR: Hank Smith
DESIGNER/ILLUSTRATOR: Gary Klingemann

DESIGN FIRM: Richland Design Associates, Cambridge, Massachusetts

ART DIRECTOR: Judith Richland

DESIGNER: Timothy Preston

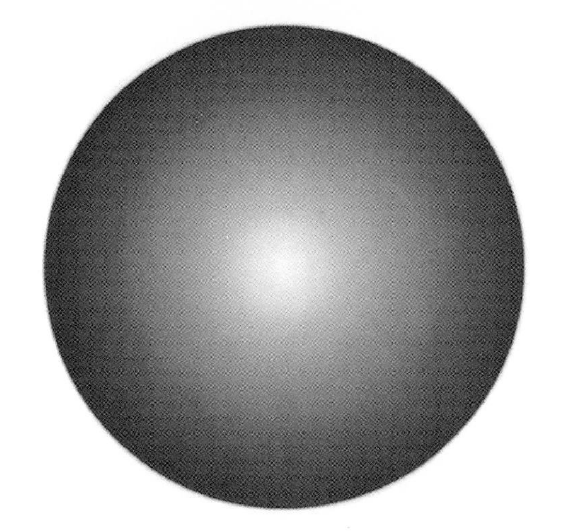

On Technology

ON TECHNOLOGY, INC.

One Cambridge Center, Suite 902 Cambridge, Massachusetts 02142 Telephone (617) 225-2545

ON TECHNOLOGY, INC.

One Cambridge Center, Suite 902
Cambridge, Massachusetts 02142

ON TECHNOLOGY, INC.

Elaine Yeomelakis
Executive Secretary

One Cambridge Center, Cambridge, MA 02142
Tel: (617) 225-2545 Fax: (617) 225-2347

ECLIPSE®

LOF Glass

DESIGN FIRM: Marketing Communications Group, Inc., Toledo, Ohio

ART DIRECTOR/ DESIGNER: Jeff Kimble

COPYWRITERS: David Horn, Greg Otis

ACCOUNT SUPERVISOR: Mary Quain

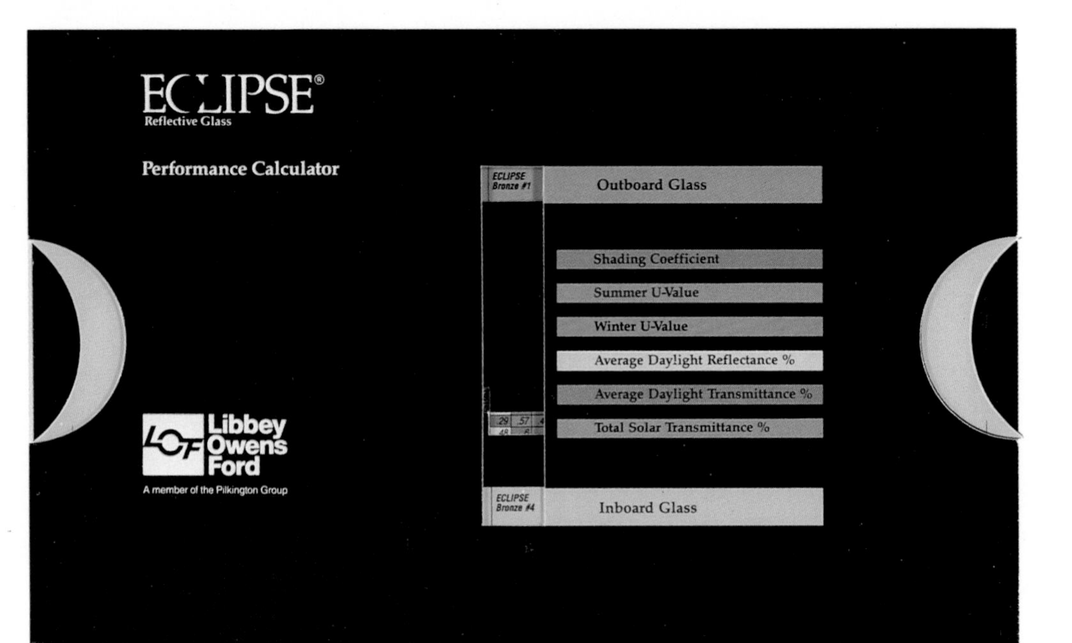

Robert J. Buzzeo Inc.
Post Office Box 105
Chichester, NY 12416
914-688-7589

Robert J. Buzzeo Inc.
Post Office Box 105
Chichester, NY 12416

Robert J. Buzzeo Inc.
Post Office Box 105
Chichester, NY 12416
914-688-7589

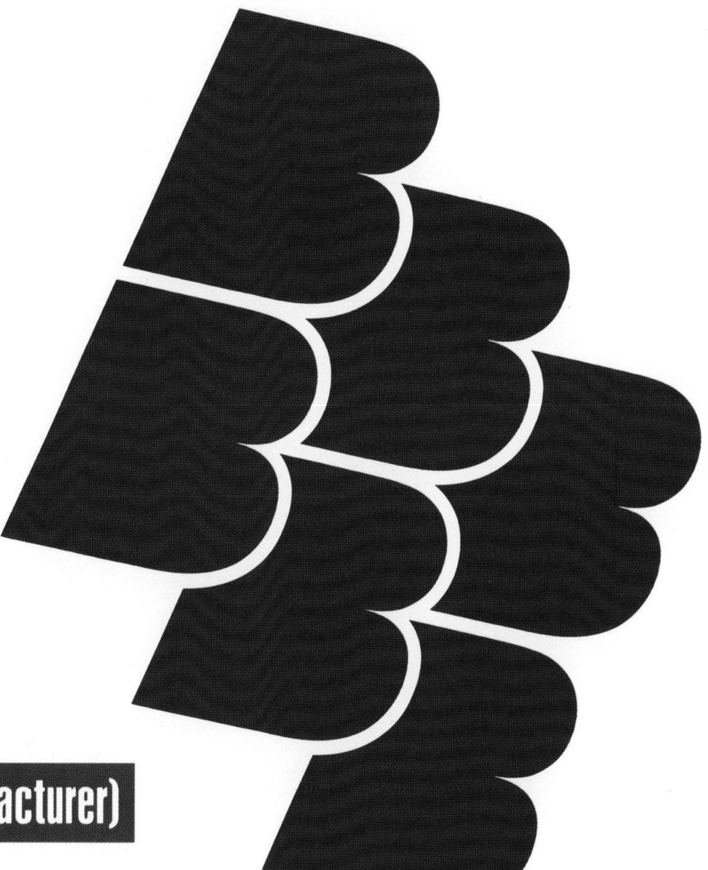

DESIGN FIRM: Jack Hough Associates, Inc., New York, New York

ART DIRECTOR: Jack Hough

DESIGNER: Chris Hough

Robert J. Buzzeo, Inc. (Wood Shingle Manufacturer)

Smith and Company
Real Estate Investment
Development Corporation

P.O. Box 283
San Luis Obispo, CA 93406
805/544-7343

Smith and Company
Real Estate Investment
Development Corporation

P.O. Box 283
San Luis Obispo, CA 93406

DESIGN FIRM: Pierre Rademaker Design, San Luis Obispo, California
ART DIRECTOR: Pierre Rademaker
DESIGNERS: Pierre Rademaker, Lori Powell

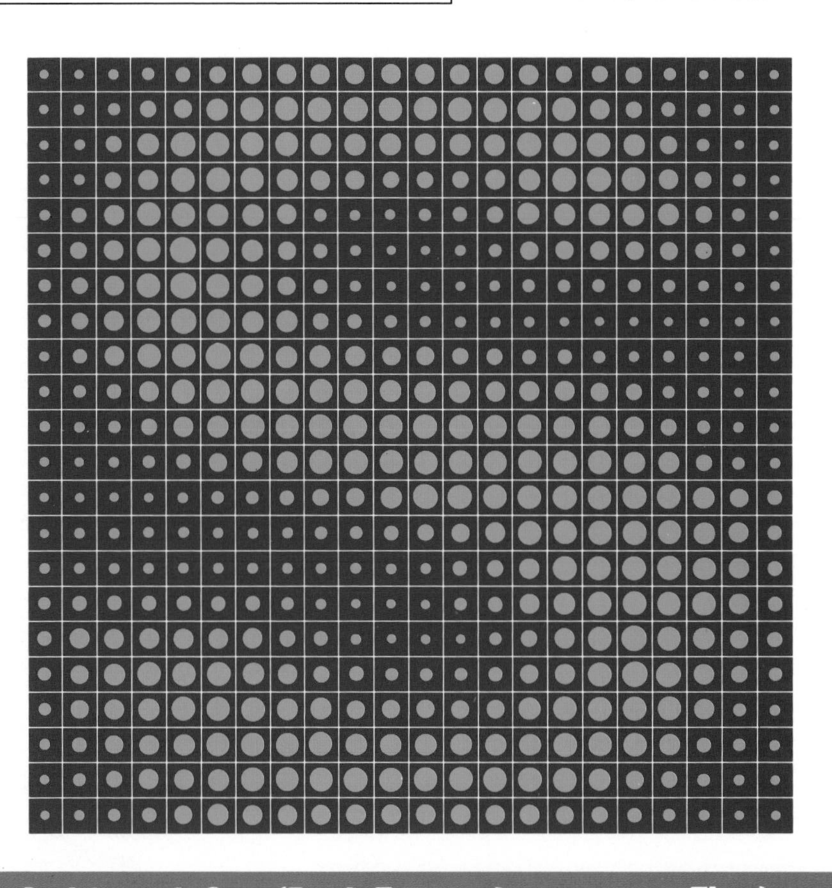

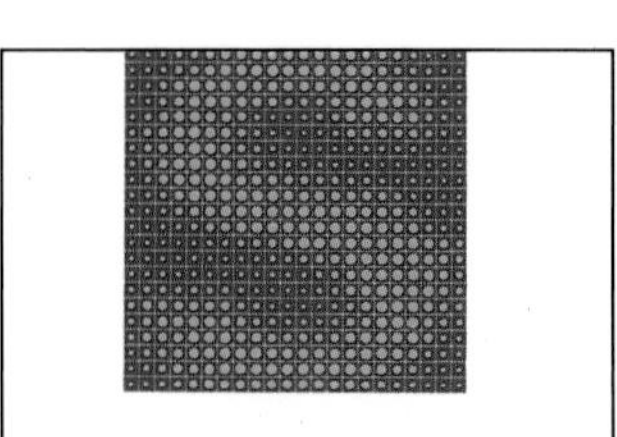

Smith and Company
Real Estate Investment
Development Corporation

Sandra L. Naumann
President's Assistant

P.O. Box 283
San Luis Obispo, CA 93406
805/544-7343

Smith and Co. (Real Estate Investment Firm)

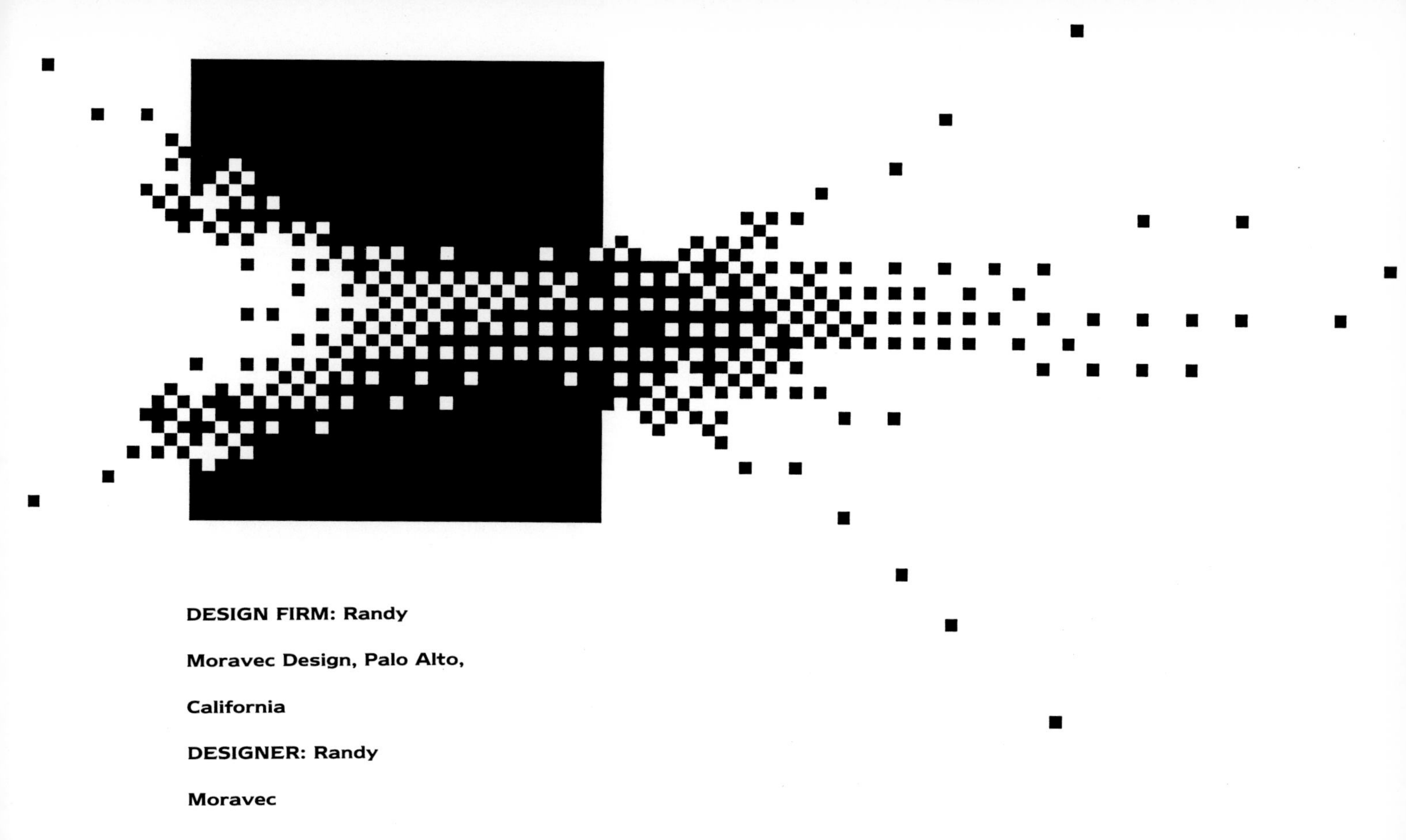

DESIGN FIRM: Randy Moravec Design, Palo Alto, California

DESIGNER: Randy Moravec

Q.E.D. Technology

DESIGN FIRM: SWA Group, Sausalito, California
DESIGNER: Bonnie Phippen

Picnics (Gourmet Delicatessen)

DESIGN FIRM: Crouch and Fuller, Inc., A Design Group West Company, Del Mar, California
ART DIRECTORS: Jim Crouch, Craig Fuller
DESIGNERS: Julian Naranjo, Craig Fuller

San Diego Padres

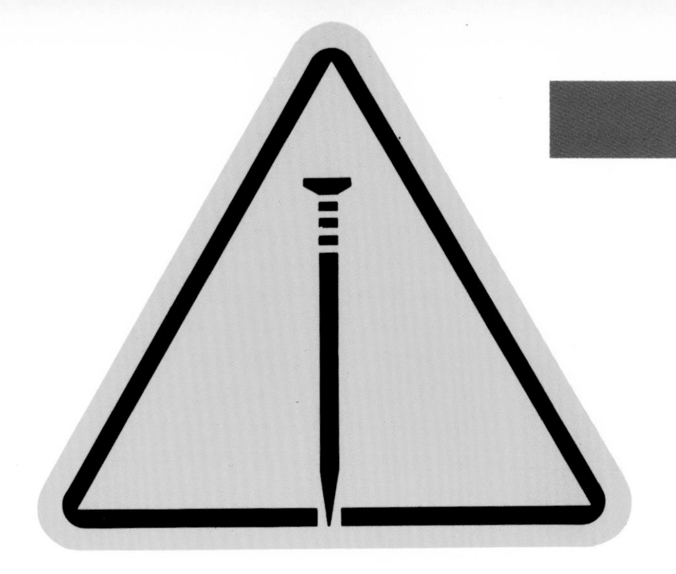

Florida Fixtures

DESIGN FIRM: Anderson Studios, Fort Lauderdale, Florida

DESIGNER: Pamela Anderson

Daylong Island (Theme Park)

DESIGN FIRM: Petree Graphics, McLean, Virginia

DESIGNER: Deborah DePrete

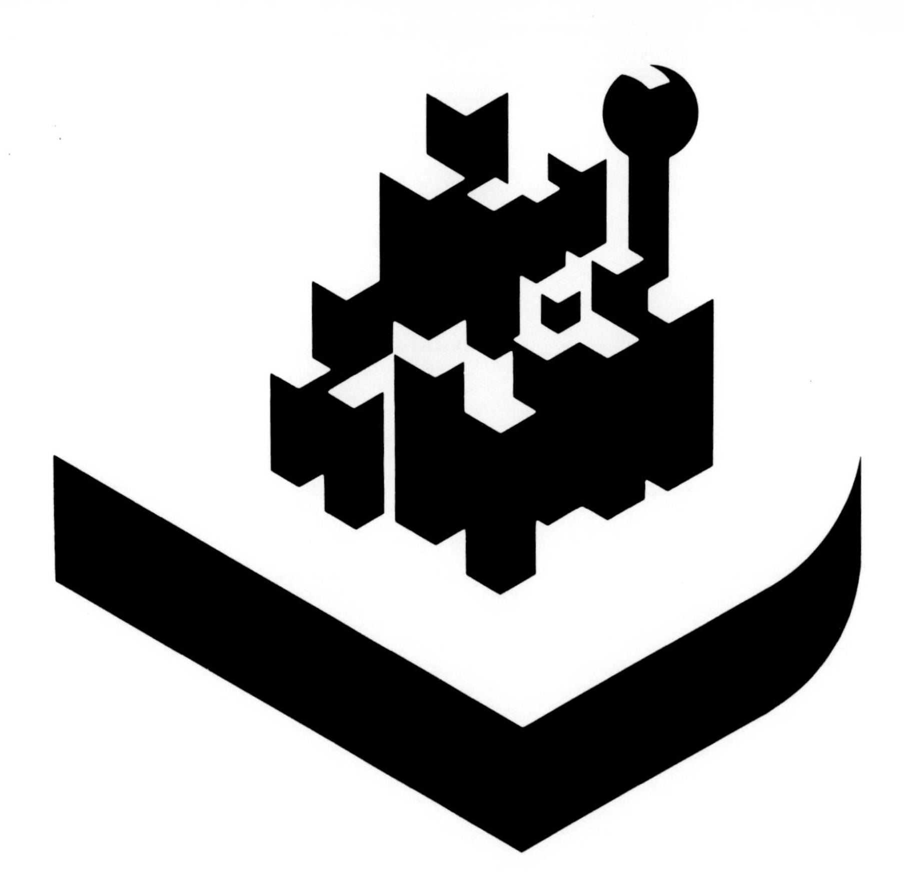

Dallas Central Business District Association

DESIGN FIRM: Eisenberg, Inc., Dallas, Texas

DESIGNER: Don Arday

DALLAS CENTRAL
BUSINESS DISTRICT
ASSOCIATION

1507 Pacific Avenue
Suite 1310
Dallas, Texas 75201-3401
214/747-8555

OFFICERS
John T. Stuart
Chairman
Henry Gilchrist
Chairman-Elect
James A. Cloar
President
James Gardner
Secretary-Treasurer

LAKE CREEK
CONSTRUCTION
INCORPORATED

BRENT
COBURN

5658
LAKE
CREEK
ROAD
HEBER
CITY,
UTAH
84032
S.L.C.
484-6383
HEBER
654-1431

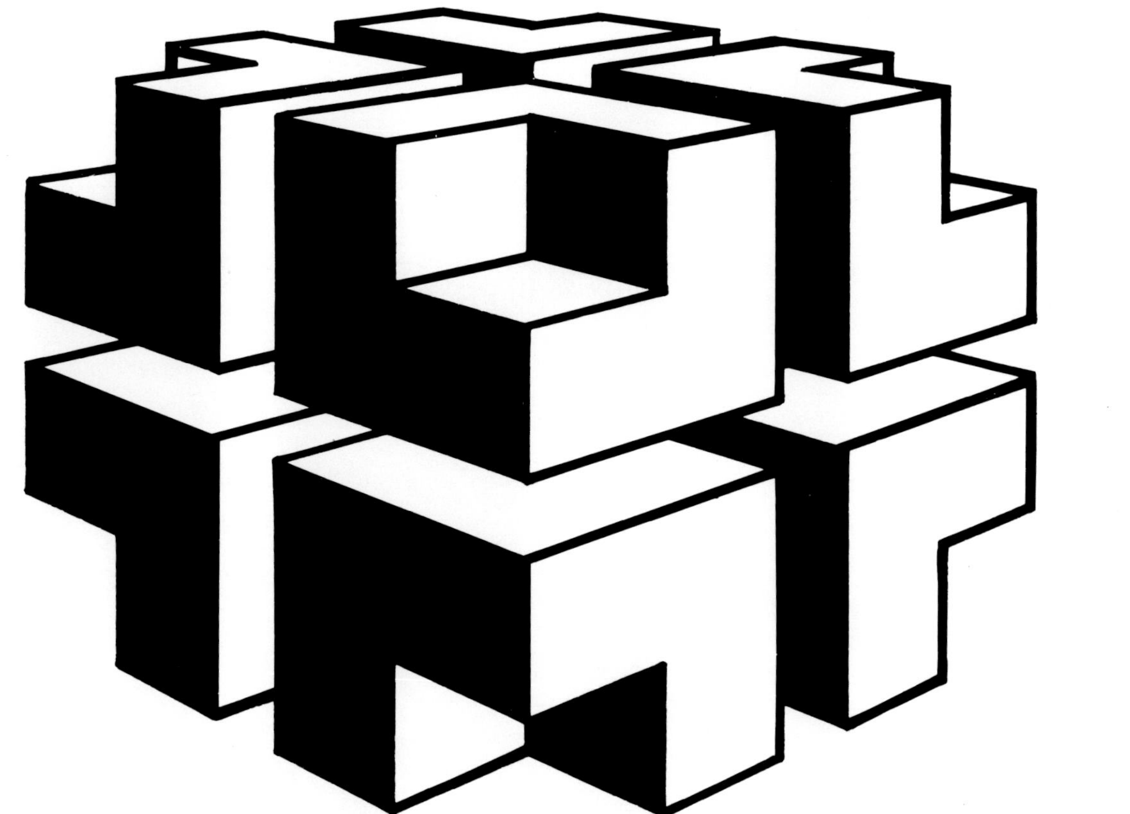

DESIGN FIRM: Royter Snow Design, Salt Lake City, Utah

ART DIRECTOR/DESIGNER: Randall Royter

Lake Creek Construction

INA/AETNA Partnership Insurance Agents

DESIGN FIRM: Kramer Miller Lomden Glassman, Philadelphia, Pennsylvania
ART DIRECTOR: Joseph Kramer
DESIGNER: Joseph Kramer, Carol Whitman

Galardi's Pizza

DESIGN FIRM: Patrick Soohoo Designers, Los Angeles, California

ART DIRECTOR: Patrick Soohoo

DESIGNER: Katherine Lam

Players Theatre of Columbus (Performance of *Benefactors*)

DESIGN FIRM: Rickabaugh Graphics, Columbus, Ohio

DESIGNERS: Eric Rickabaugh, John Smith

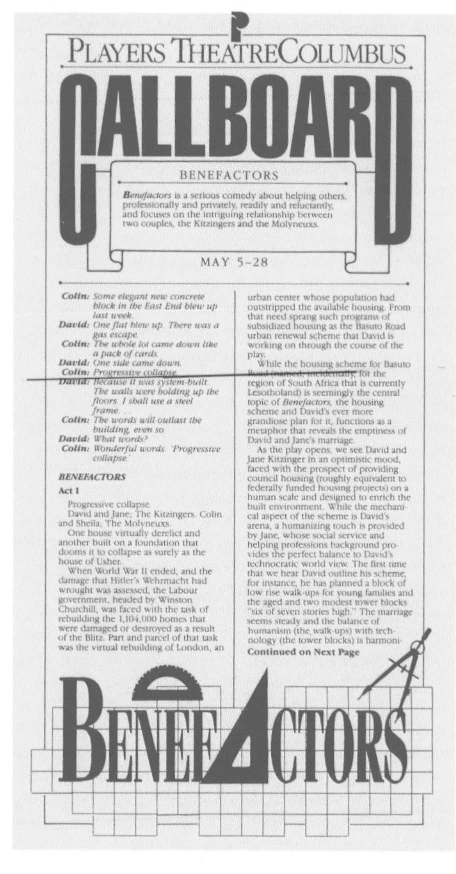

PLAYERS THEATRECOLUMBUS

CALLBOARD

BENEFACTORS

Benefactors is a serious comedy about helping others, professionally and privately, readily and reluctantly, and focuses on the intriguing relationship between two couples, the Kitzingers and the Molyneuxs.

MAY 5–28

Colin: *Some elegant new concrete block in the East End blew up last week.*
David: *One flat blew up. There was a gas escape.*
Colin: *The whole lot came down like a pack of cards.*
David: *One side came down.*
Colin: *Progressive collapse.*
David: *Because it was system-built. The walls were holding up the floors. I shall use a steel frame. . .*
Colin: *The words will outlast the building, even so.*
David: *What words?*
Colin: *Wonderful words. 'Progressive collapse.'*

BENEFACTORS

Act 1

Progressive collapse.

David and Jane; The Kitzingers. Colin and Sheila; The Molyneuxs.

One house virtually derelict and another built on a foundation that dooms it to collapse as surely as the house of Usher.

When World War II ended, and the damage that Hitler's Wehrmacht had wrought was assessed, the Labour government, headed by Winston Churchill, was faced with the task of rebuilding the 1,104,000 homes that were damaged or destroyed as a result of the Blitz. Part and parcel of that task was the virtual rebuilding of London, an urban center whose population had outstripped the available housing. From that need sprang such programs of subsidized housing as the Basuto Road urban renewal scheme that David is working on through the course of the play.

While the housing scheme for Basuto Road (named, incidentally, for the region of South Africa that is currently Lesotholand) is seemingly the central topic of *Benefactors*, the housing scheme and David's ever more grandiose plan for it, functions as a metaphor that reveals the emptiness of David and Jane's marriage.

As the play opens, we see David and Jane Kitzinger in an optimistic mood, faced with the prospect of providing council housing (roughly equivalent to federally funded housing projects) on a human scale and designed to enrich the built environment. While the mechanical aspect of the scheme is David's arena, a humanizing touch is provided by Jane, whose social service and helping professions background provides the perfect balance to David's technocratic world view. The first time that we hear David outline his scheme, for instance, he has planned a block of low rise walk-ups for young families and the aged and two modest tower blocks "six of seven stories high." The marriage seems steady and the balance of humanism (the walk-ups) with technology (the tower blocks) is harmoni-

Continued on Next Page

BENEFACTORS

Southland Shopping Center

DESIGN FIRM: Petro Graphic Design Associates, Rocky River, Ohio

DESIGNER/ILLUSTRATOR: Nancy Bero Petro

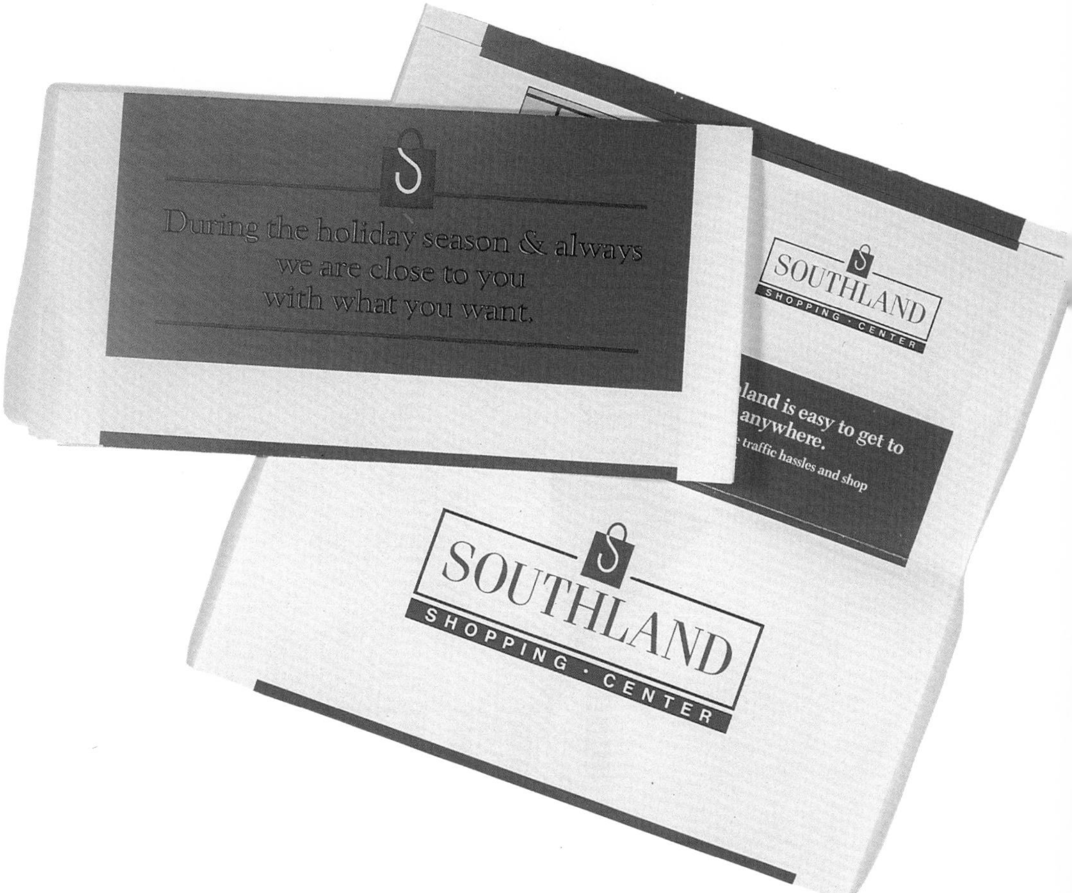

SOUTHLAND

SHOPPING · CENTER

Hot Heads

DESIGN FIRM: Ads, Inc., Milwaukee, Wisconsin
ART DIRECTOR: Ken Eichenbaum
DESIGNER: Rich Kohnke
ILLUSTRATOR: Dave Schweitzer

THERESE
& COMPANY

DESIGN FIRM: Mitchell Creative, Memphis, Tennessee
CREATIVE DIRECTOR/ DESIGNER: Chuck Mitchell
ART DIRECTOR/ ILLUSTRATOR: Beth Robinson Mitchell

Therese & Company (Children's and Teen's Clothing)

Red Rooster Restaurants

DESIGN FIRM: Bruce Hale Design Studios, Seattle, Washington

DESIGNER: Bruce Hale

Palmetto Products

DESIGN FIRM: Lesniewicz/ Navarre, Toledo, Ohio

DESIGNER: Terry Lesniewicz

Plano Crisis Center

DESIGN FIRM: Eisenberg, Inc., Dallas, Texas

ART DIRECTORS: Scott Ray, Arthur Eisenberg

DESIGNER: Scott Ray

PLANO CRISIS
CENTER, INC.

P.O. Box 1808
Plano, Texas 75074
214-881-0088

Board Members
Glenn Weimer, PH.D.
Chris Roach, M.D.
Ann Stokes
Val Sharp
Glenda May
Alex Williams
Ruth Steenbergen
Francis Reyna
Celia Oliphant
Bill Galloway
Judy Mouden
Kay Kramme
Rich Fulkerson
Carla Bateman
Ivy Spina

DESIGNER/ILLUSTRATOR:

Barbara Richied,

Minneapolis, Minnesota

Planet Pictures

Rancho dos Cañadas

DESIGN FIRM: Knoth & Meads, San Diego, California

ART DIRECTOR/ DESIGNER: José Serrano

ILLUSTRATOR: Tracy Sabin

DESIGNER/ILLUSTRATOR:

Anne DeSantis, San José, California

SAN JOSÉ
SYMPHONY
ORCHESTRA

Friday, December 5, 1986, 8:30 p.m.
Saturday, December 6, 1986, 8:30 p.m.
San Jose Center for the Performing Arts

Sunday, December 7, 1986, 2:30 p.m.
Flint Center, De Anza College, Cupertino

George Cleve, *Conductor*
Jacalyn Bower, *Mezzo-soprano*

Antonin Dvorák
(1841-1904)

Serenade in D minor, Op. 44
Moderato quasi marcia
Menuetto-Trio: Presto
Andante con moto
Finale: Allegro molto

Maurice Ravel
(1875-1937)

Shéhérazade
Asie
La Flûte enchantée
L'Indifférént
Jacalyn Bower, ***Mezzo-soprano***

INTERMISSION

Johannes Brahms
(1833-1897)

Symphony No. 4 in E minor, Op. 98
Allegro non troppo
Andante moderato
Allegro giocoso
Allegro energico e passionato

These concerts are sponsored in part by a generous grant from Wells Fargo Bank

XIX

BODY BEAUTIFUL

Body Beautiful (A Weight Reduction Studio)

DESIGN FIRM: Steven Sessions, Inc., Houston, Texas

ART DIRECTOR/ DESIGNER: Steven Sessions

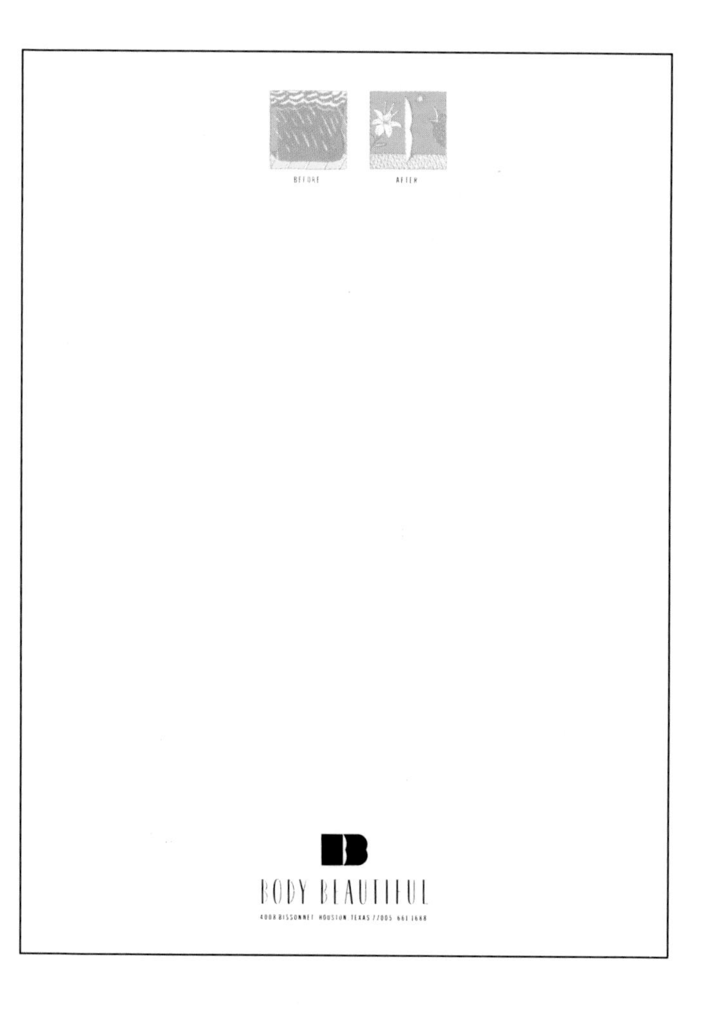

PLAYERS THEATRECOLUMBUS

CALLBOARD

OPENING NIGHT CELEBRATION! (SEE DETAILS INSIDE)

A MURDER OF CROWS

A gleaming story of honor, family, midwest pride, and legacy. Set in a farming village in Ohio, the story centers around Woodson's Store, a combination grocery, post office, and bus stop. Harley and Jennie are being forced to leave their home, facing certain death from a nearby toxic waste site. Their son Corey, with his wife Doris, has returned home to collect his parents, share memories, and examine their relationships.

SEPTEMBER 24-OCTOBER 18

Ed Graczyk, Producing Director of Players TheatreColumbus, whose play *A Murder of Crows* will open Players 1987-1988 season, took time recently to talk with Hugh Murphy about the play and about playwrighting in general.

HUGH MURPHY—The play, A Murder of Crows, *exists in an almost timeless void. There are very few references that are topical, or that tie the play to a certain time. Is there a reason for that?*

ED GRACZYK—Audrey Wood once said to me that the best plays are those that are 'timeless.' *Streetcar Named Desire* is timeless. *Death of a Salesman* is timeless. I think that it's the people and the situations that matter. When you start dealing with universal themes, there are themes that can exist at any time. Because of that comment of Audrey's, I'm probably conscious of that as I write. I want to create a period of time and show what has happened—as with *Enemy of the People.* It talks about the effects on time, the people of that time. I want this one to talk about this time, but go beyond this

HM—Since you've mentioned other playwrights—as I read Murder, *I got echoes of O'Neill, particularly* Moon for the Misbegotten. *I heard here and there a turn of phrase that made me think of Romulus Linney or Lanford Wilson. How cognizant are you, as a playwright, of other writers?*

EG—I think that O'Neill, Inge (who is very much a favorite playwright of mine), some Tennessee Williams (although not as much), and Lanford Wilson are all naturalist playwrights writing about particular types of people. *The Iceman Cometh, Moon for the Misbegotten,* were all written about lower middle class, blue collar people. Inge's people were all working class Kansas. I think only in that respect does the play have echoes. I'm not sure that I'm that aware of other playwrights, as I am aware of a strong feeling of place. When I wrote the play, I *was* in Wallace, Ohio. **Continued on Next Page.**

THE WORLD PREMIERE

A MURDER OF CROWS

DESIGN FIRM: Rickabaugh Graphics, Columbus, Ohio

DESIGNER: Eric Rickabaugh

ILLUSTRATORS: Eric Rickabaugh, John Smith

Oliver Ranch

DESIGN FIRM:

Alvin Ugay Design,

Fairfield, California

ART DIRECTOR/

DESIGNER/ILLUSTRATOR:

Alvin Ugay

OLIVER RANCH

Green Thumb Plant Store

DESIGN FIRM: Steven Sessions, Inc., Houston, Texas

ART DIRECTOR/ DESIGNER: Steven Sessions

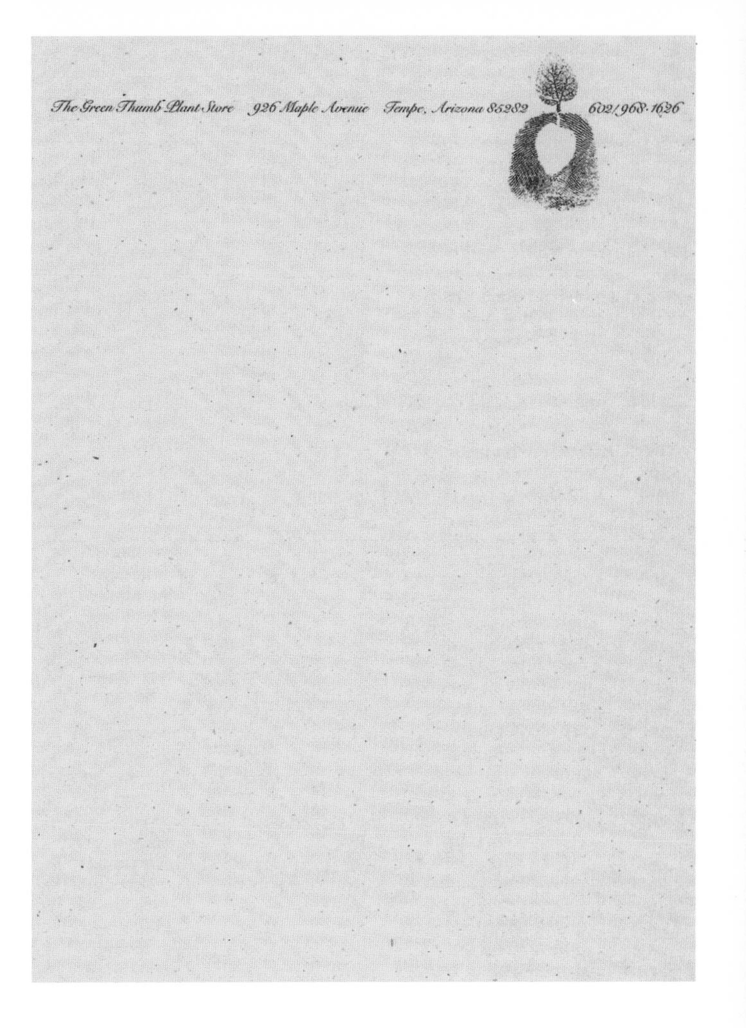

Speaking of Fitness

A health and exercise speakers association.
DESIGN FIRM: Studio Bustamante, San Diego, California
DESIGNER/ILLUSTRATOR: Gerald Bustamante

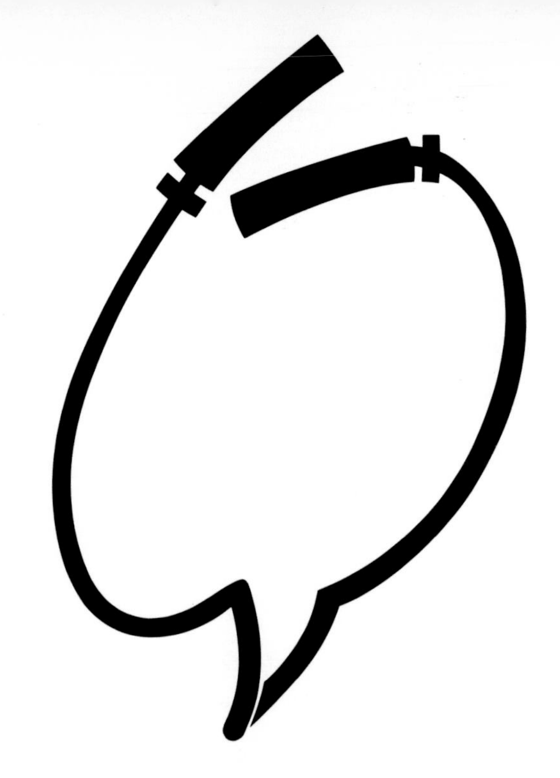

Alliance Theater

Atlanta, Georgia, gift-giving campaign.
DESIGN FIRM: Ray's Seefood, Auburn, Alabama
ART DIRECTOR: Tazewell S. Morton (Rafshoon Advertising)
DESIGNER/ILLUSTRATOR: Ray B. Dugas

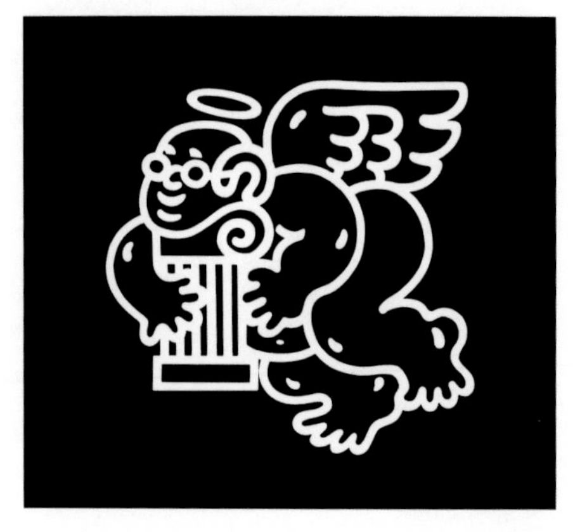

National Guild of the Arts

DESIGN FIRM: Kramer Miller Lomden Glassman, Philadelphia, Pennsylvania
DESIGNER: Ted Miller

Sumiko's Hairstyling

DESIGNER/ILLUSTRATOR: Mel Hioki, New York, New York

SUMIKO'S HAIRSTYLING

Digits (Manufacturer of Finger Watches)

DESIGN FIRM: Jackson Design, Nashville, Tennessee
CREATIVE DIRECTOR/ DESIGNER: Buddy Jackson

DIGITS™

Marine Midland (Auto Finance)

DESIGN FIRM: Duffy Design Group, Minneapolis, Minnesota

ART DIRECTOR/ ILLUSTRATOR: Charles S. Anderson

DESIGNERS: Charles S. Anderson, Sharon Werner

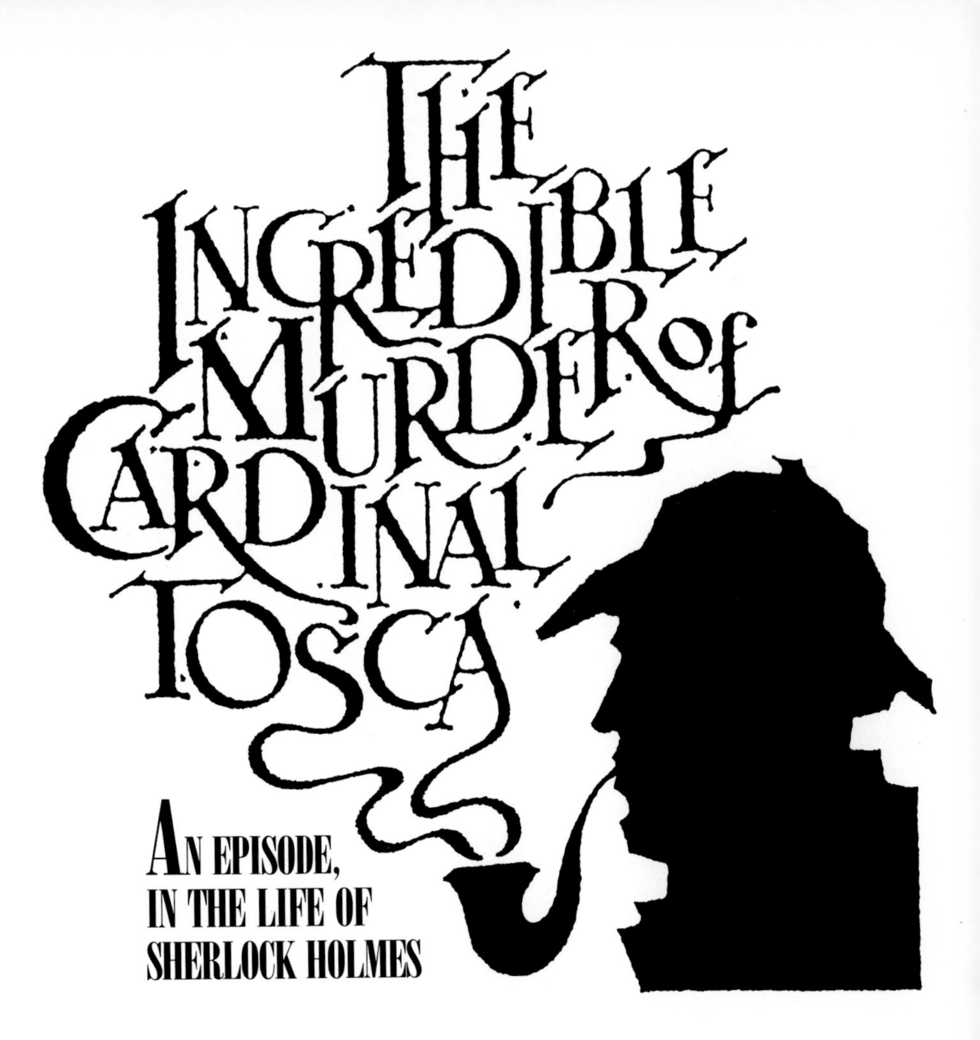

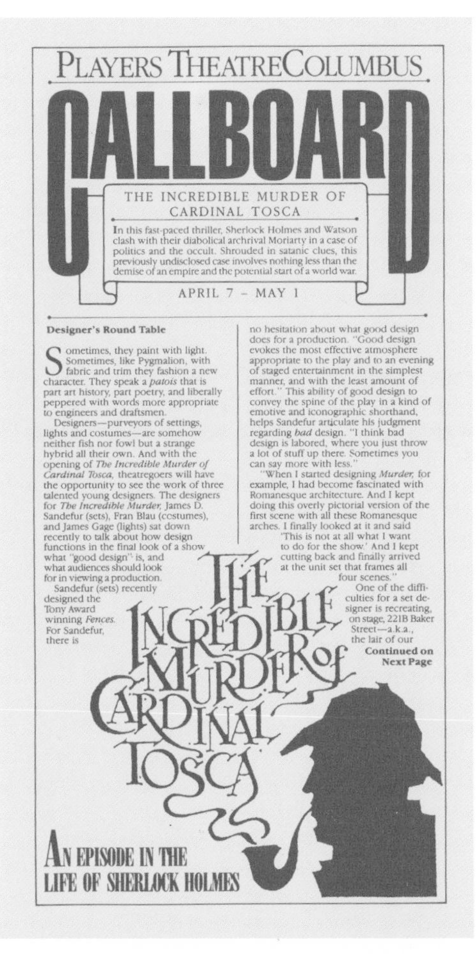

PLAYERS THEATRE COLUMBUS

CALLBOARD

THE INCREDIBLE MURDER OF CARDINAL TOSCA

In this fast-paced thriller, Sherlock Holmes and Watson clash with their diabolical archrival Moriarty in a case of politics and the occult. Shrouded in satanic clues, this previously undisclosed case involves nothing less than the demise of an empire and the potential start of a world war.

APRIL 7 – MAY 1

Designer's Round Table

Sometimes, they paint with light. Sometimes, like Pygmalion, with fabric and trim they fashion a new character. They speak a *patois* that is part art history, part poetry, and liberally peppered with words more appropriate to engineers and draftsmen.

Designers—purveyors of settings, lights and costumes—are somehow neither fish nor fowl but a strange hybrid all their own. And with the opening of *The Incredible Murder of Cardinal Tosca*, theatregoers will have the opportunity to see the work of three talented young designers. The designers for *The Incredible Murder*, James D. Sandefur (sets), Fran Blau (costumes), and James Gage (lights) sat down recently to talk about how design functions in the final look of a show what "good design" is, and what audiences should look for in viewing a production.

Sandefur (sets) recently designed the Tony Award winning *Fences*. For Sandefur, there is no hesitation about what good design does for a production. "Good design evokes the most effective atmosphere appropriate to the play and to an evening of staged entertainment in the simplest manner, and with the least amount of effort." This ability of good design to convey the spine of the play in a kind of emotive and iconographic shorthand, helps Sandefur articulate his judgment regarding *bad* design. "I think bad design is labored, where you just throw a lot of stuff up there. Sometimes you can say more with less."

"When I started designing *Murder*, for example, I had become fascinated with Romanesque architecture. And I kept doing this overly pictorial version of the first scene with all these Romanesque arches. I finally looked at it and said 'This is not at all what I want to do for the show.' And I kept cutting back and finally arrived at the unit set that frames all four scenes."

One of the difficulties for a set designer is recreating, on stage, 221B Baker Street—a.k.a., the lair of our

Continued on Next Page

THE INCREDIBLE MURDER OF CARDINAL TOSCA

AN EPISODE IN THE LIFE OF SHERLOCK HOLMES

DESIGN FIRM: Rickabaugh Graphics, Columbus, Ohio

ART DIRECTOR: Eric Rickabaugh

ILLUSTRATORS: Eric Rickabaugh, John Smith

Players Theatre of Columbus (Performance of *The Incredible Murder of Cardinal Tosca*)

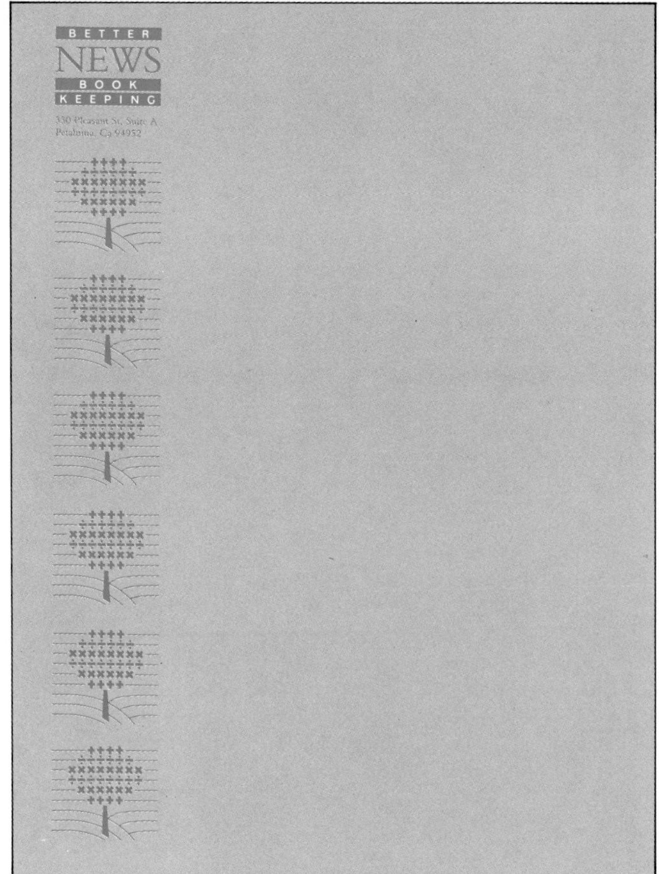

Better Bookkeeping

DESIGN FIRM: Grey Visual, Cotati, California

ART DIRECTOR/ DESIGNER: William Grey

ILLUSTRATOR: Cynthia Brush

Specialty Press

DESIGN FIRM: Geer Design, Inc., Houston, Texas

ART DIRECTOR/ DESIGNER: Mark Geer, Richard Kilmer

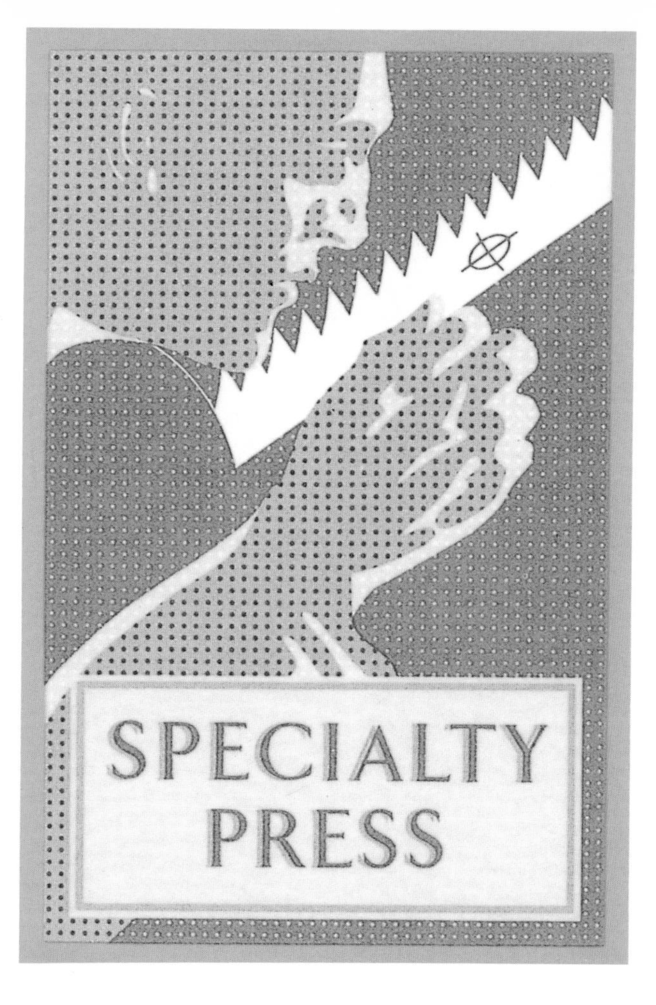

JOE PORTELE

8520 SWEETWATER
SUITE C-22
HOUSTON, TEXAS 77037
713 999 2717

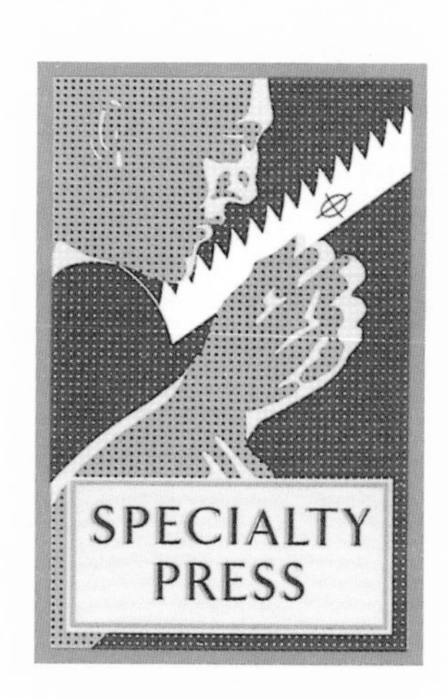

8520 SWEETWATER
SUITE C-22
HOUSTON, TEXAS 77037
713 999 2717

ORIENTATIONS

Orientations (Travel Consultants)

DESIGN FIRM: David J. Baca Design Associates, San José, California
ART DIRECTOR/ DESIGNER/ILLUSTRATOR: David J. Baca

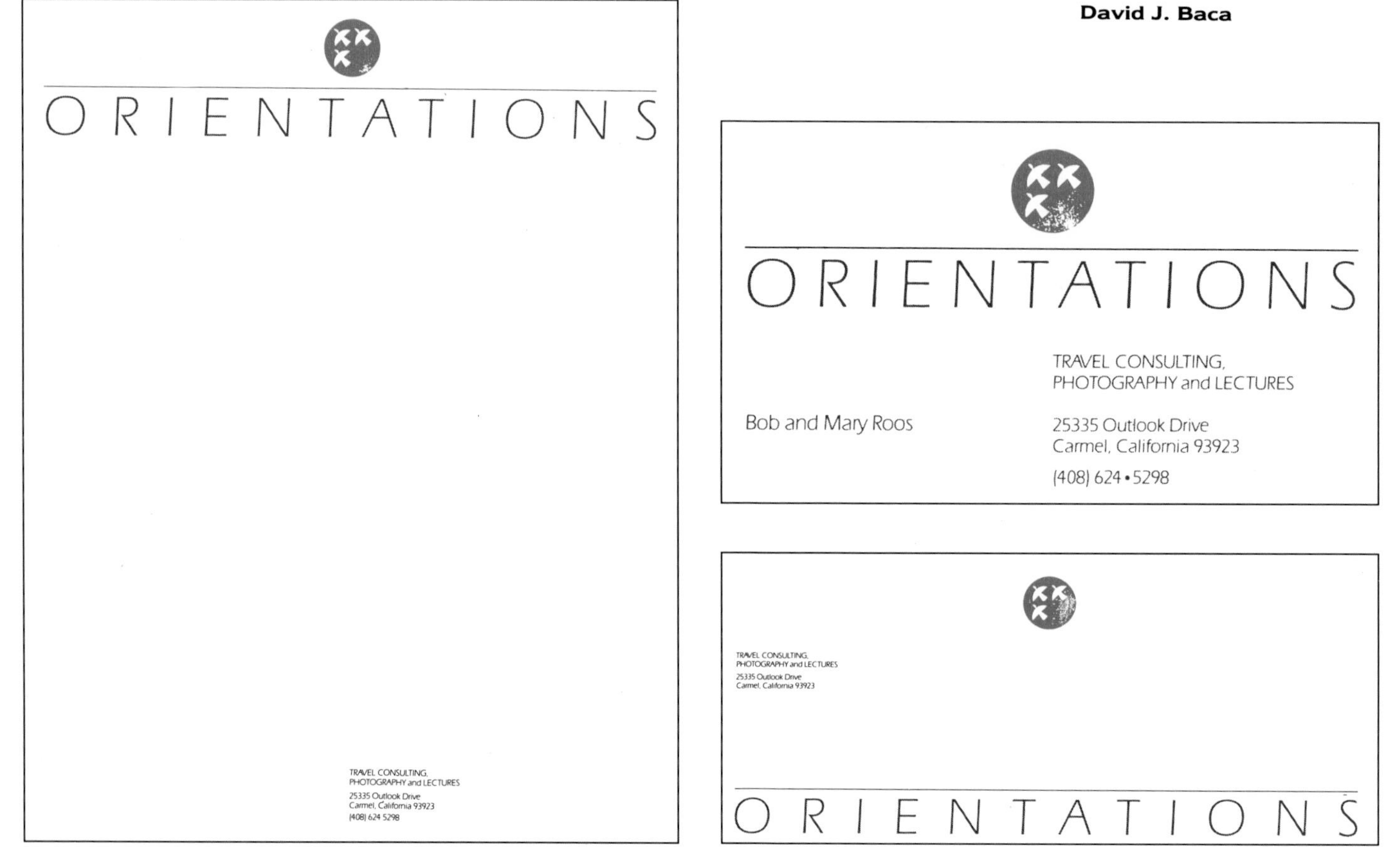

Tucson Art Expo

DESIGN FIRM: Boelts Bros. Design, Inc., Tucson, Arizona

ART DIRECTORS/ DESIGNERS/ PHOTOGRAPHERS: Jackson Boelts, Eric Boelts

Mobile Infirmary

DESIGNER: Lynne Wells, Decatur, Alabama

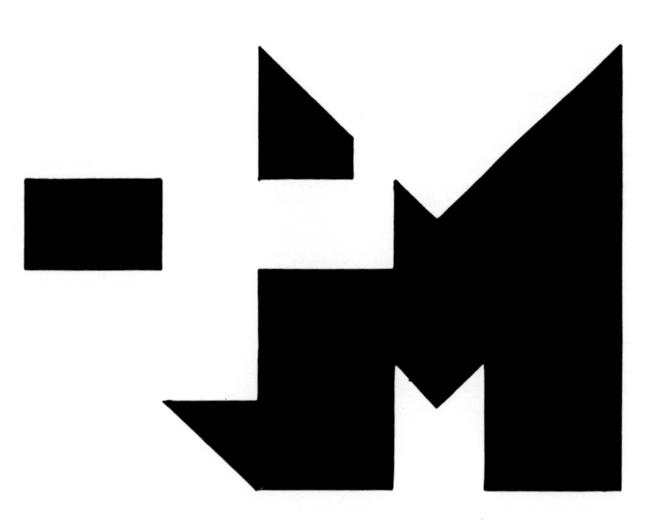

Lighten Up

A Stanford University weight-loss program.

DESIGN FIRM: Hegstrom Design, Campbell, California

ART DIRECTOR/ ILLUSTRATOR: John Stoneham

DESIGNER: Ken Hegstrom

Third National Bank

DESIGN FIRM: Jennifer Closner Design, Minneapolis, Minnesota

DESIGNER: Jennifer Closner

Young Republicans

DESIGN FIRM: Grimsrud Publishing, Inc., Zumbrota, Minnesota

DESIGNER: David A. Grimsrud

Alcoholism and Drug Treatment Center

DESIGN FIRM: Carol Kerr Graphic Design, San Diego, California

ART DIRECTOR: Carol Kerr

DESIGNER/ILLUSTRATOR: Eric Olson

Hilden + Hahn Photography

DESIGN FIRM: Rod Brown Design, Dallas, Texas

CREATIVE DIRECTOR/ART DIRECTOR: Rod Brown

DESIGNER/ILLUSTRATOR: T. Scott Stromberg

Taverna Christina

DESIGN FIRM: Eisenberg, Inc., Dallas, Texas

ART DIRECTORS: Arthur Eisenberg, Scott Ray

DESIGNER: Scott Ray

ILLUSTRATORS: Curtis Asplund, Scott Ray

INDEX

CLIENTS

DESIGN FIRMS

ART DIRECTORS/DESIGNERS